Dedication

To my Family, Ruthie, Gabrielle, Ariel, Micael, my mother, and all those who supported me along this marathon of investing, thank you.

I am grateful in having the opportunity to work with and build a wonderful team of colleagues from the Kramer brothers, to Rob & Chris, to my solicitor Pamela, my accountant David always there to answer my myriad of questions, our architect Ric who has guided us through the maze of council regulations as well as all of our loyal building teams. None of the successes in this book could not have been achieved without the dedicated and hard work of all of the team....

Huge Thank you for making it all possible!!!

www.bhinvestment.co.uk

Risk Disclosure

Limit of Liability/Disclaimer of Warranty:

While the author has used his best efforts in preparing this book, he makes no representations or warranties with respect to the accuracy or completeness of the contents of this book and specifically disclaims any implied warranties of merchantability or fitness for a particular purpose. No warranty may be created or extended by sales representatives or written sales materials. The advice and strategies contained herein may not be suitable for your situation. You should consult with a professional where appropriate. Neither the publisher nor author shall be liable for any loss of profit or any other commercial damages, including but not limited to special, incidental, consequential, or other damages.

All material in this eBook is of my own personal opinions and not to taken as investment advice. I personally have been investing in real estate through out my life and want to share my own personal thoughts. If you have any doubt about the suitability of any of my personal opinions or you require financial advice, you should seek a personal recommendation from an appropriately qualified financial advisor that does give advice.

An investment in property contains risks. You may not get the returns expected and your capital is at risk. Your investment in property should only be considered as part of a diverse portfolio which contains investments of different kinds and where you do not put too great a proportion of your capital into one particular type of investment. The market value of property can go down as well as up and the return of your capital would be dependent on a sale of a property which is not guaranteed.

We are not regulated by the Financial Conduct Authority and does not offer any advice about any regulated or unregulated investments either within this document or elsewhere. The content of this document has not been approved by an authorized person within the meaning of the Financial Services and Markets Act 2000 (the Act). Our products are not regulated investments for the purposes of the

Act and as such buyers have no access to statutory or regulatory protections such as the Financial Ombudsman Service and the Financial Services Compensation Scheme. This is not in any way an offer to participate in a collective investment scheme (CIS) as defined in section 235 of the Act.

This document is not a recommendation or offer to provide investment services or advice to acquire or dispose of any investment or to engage in any other transaction. Nothing in this document constitutes a solicitation, invitation or inducement to engage in investment activity of any kind under section 21 of the Act. The provision of the information in this document does not constitute an offer to purchase an investment to any person in any jurisdiction. This document is provided for information purposes only and is not intended for distribution to, or use by, any person or entity resident or domiciled in, or any citizen of, any jurisdiction or country where such distribution or use would be contrary to law or regulation or would subject us or any of our affiliates, officers or employees to any registration requirement.

All rights reserved. No part of this publication may be reproduced, distributed, or transmitted in any form or by any means, including photocopying, recording, or other electronic or mechanical methods, without the prior written permission of the publisher, except in the case of brief quotations embodied in critical reviews and certain other noncommercial uses permitted by copyright law

Table of Contents

Dedication

Risk Disclosure

Preface
    Who is this book for
    Certain is Uncertain
    £ Has been Pounded
    Frozen Investor Monies in Commercial Funds
    Remembering Northern Rock
    Stock Market Volatility
    Bond Funds & Interest Rate Returns
    Is it Worth the Risk?

My Story

Why Manchester?

Profiting from the Brexit

Property Investment Strategies -Brexit or Not

    My personal real estate strategies
    What I completely avoid
    Boring Terraced Housing investing
    Real World Examples of Terraced Housing Investing
    Time for Cheeky offers?

Crisis investing from Legendary Billionaires

Increasing your Profits with Houses of Multiple Occupation
    Real Deals

Professional Tenanted HMOs

Commercial to Residential Money Machines
    Always be Creative & Enhance Value

Joint Ventures in Real Estate

Conclusion and Summary

Preface

Who is this Book For?

Actually I wrote this book in order to share with my children and help them to become independent thinkers and hopefully to assist them to be financially independent. I do not want them to follow the crowd.

The ideas I have expressed are not the HOLY GRAIL as it does not exist.

One must invest according to their own risk profile and personality.

I feel that we are in **completely unknown and turbulent times**. I am far from perfect and the ideas espoused in this book are my own and not meant in place for professional financial advice. I have included ideas from some of the worlds leading financial minds and billionaires whose credentials stand on their own. My goal is to try to assist you in prospering from the uncertainty via real estate, a field in which I have invested a great deal of my life.

The Certain is the Uncertain

The certain is that Britain has voted to leave the EU. The Brexit vote is old news. What is the new, is the complete unknown consequences. There will be short term and long term consequences.

We all witnessed that some of the world's stock markets declined by 3.6%, Oil declined by 5%, gold surged 4.4% and importantly, the 10-year U.S. Treasury rate declined by 9% from 1.74% to 1.58%, the lowest rate since 2012 immediately after the vote.

However what is now the source of countless discussions, *Where do we go from here?*

What is next?

No one knows!

Not the politicians!

Not the newspapers!

But everyone seems to have their opinions right or wrong.

The only thing is certain is the UNCERTAINTY!

Uncertainty after the referendum has started to delay both corporate as well as well as individuals decisions. Virtually all major economic decisions; such as investments, construction and housing market activity have been side tracked.

What is for sure however that Consumer confidence is **has dived at the fastest pace in more than 20 years** and the vast majority expects the economy to worsen and inflation to go up.

Inflation is a wealth destroyer. With the pound plunging it stands to reason inflation is on the immediate horizon. Discretionary spending could be cut back and sectors like travel, fashion and lifestyle, home, living, DIY and grocery. All of this has a carry over effect or domino effect.

I doubt that most really believed the so called fear mongering before the vote. However what we are experiencing "so far" has probably shocked all of us.

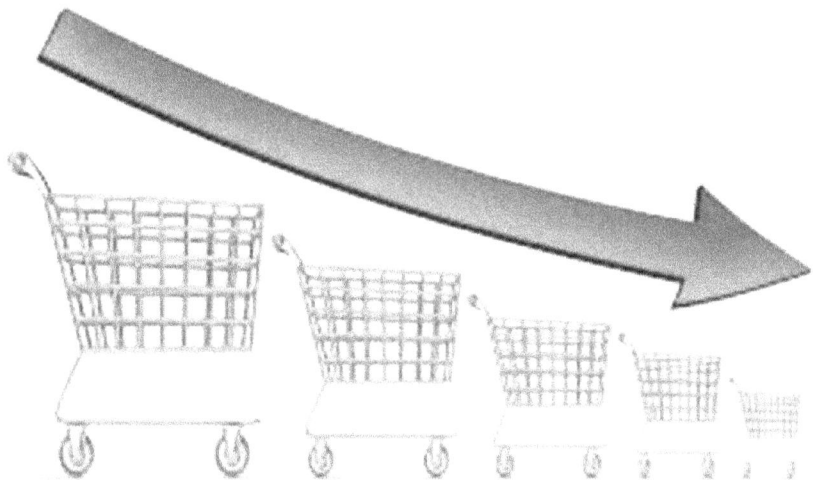

The British Pound has gotten pummeled!

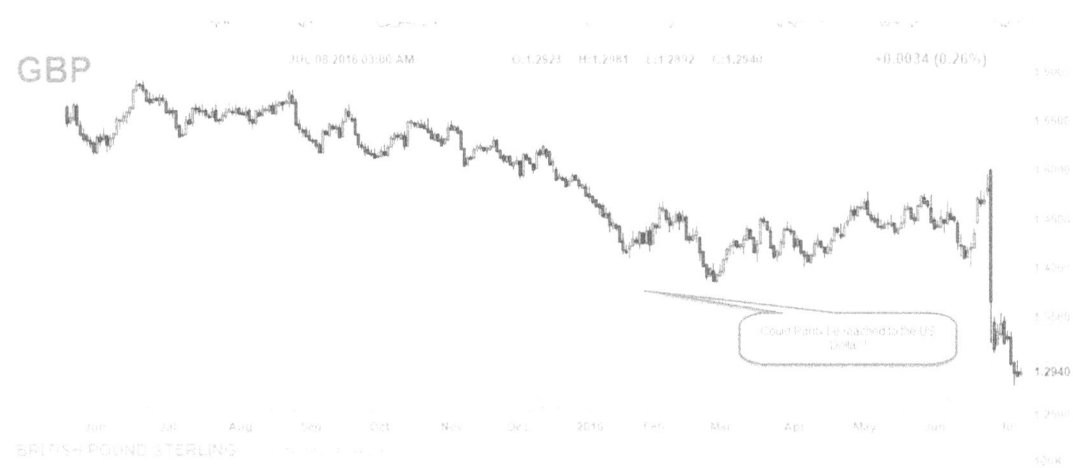

The pound tumbled to a 31-year low, crashing below $1.30, on fears over the effect of last month's Brexit vote on Britain's property market and the prospect of cuts in Bank of England interest rates. This level is the lowest level since June 1985. The British currency is considered one of the main vehicles through which financial markets can express their concern about Brexit. Chief Economic Advisor to Allianz Mohamed El-Erian said that he feels that unless the government acts rapidly to control the situation the pound could touch parity against the dollar.

OUCH!!!

So much for the vacation in Spain?

Is inflation on our door step? Are food prices going to increase? What about prices of heating and petrol?

£18 Billion of Investor funds in Commercial Property Funds Frozen!!!

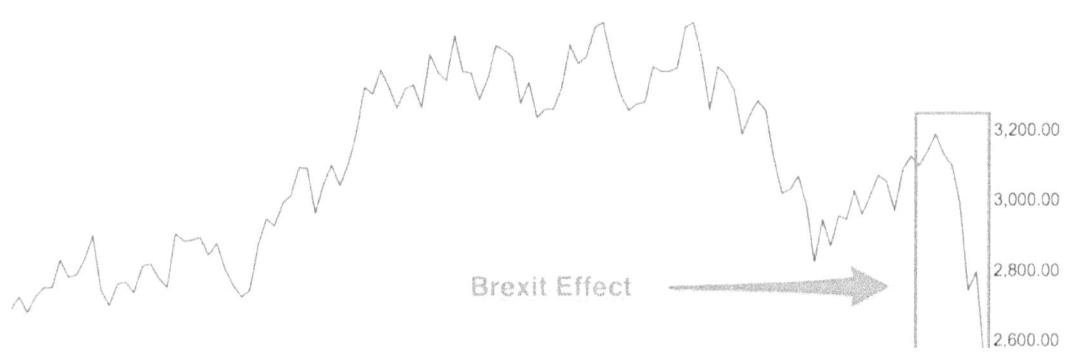

Investors were spooked and attempted to withdraw money from U.K. property funds even before the Brexit. Experts and analysts have warned that **London office values could fall by as much as 20 percent within three years of the country leaving the EU**. This created a stampede of withdrawals. However the funds fearing forced liquidations gated all redemptions or imposed draconian restrictions.

Aberdeen Fund Managers Ltd. cut the value of a property fund by 17 percent and suspended redemptions so that investors who asked for their money back have time to reconsider.

"Sure" Doesn't this scare their investors even more?

How nice of Aberdeen. Can you imagine having your pension money there?

"Shareholders wishing to redeem will do so at a price which is subject to the above dilution adjustment in order to reflect the current market environment and the fact that short-term trading in the property market has relatively penal consequences," the firm said.

Prior to the Brexit vote Aberdeen stated

"The portfolio was positioned defensively prior to the referendum with one of the highest levels of liquidity of all similar funds and having sold all its quoted property companies investments in the week prior to the referendum and holding this as cash,"

Standard Life Investments was the first money manager to halt withdrawals followed by Aviva Investors and M&G Investments. However the dominoes kept falling. Many professional and experienced investors are spooked.

Stopping redemption is however, not the answer as it will lead to more panic which can spread to other asset classes.

The ghosts of Bear Stearns and Lehman are arising.

Property funds in the past have provided an early litmus test of how great or how terrible investors are feeling right now.

The credit crisis of 2007 began with the freezing of two property funds at Bear Stearns.

The basic premises of investing are very simple and are based on confidence and perceptive tenants

Confidence that someone will buy an asset for more than you paid overtime

Confidence tenants will pay their rent

Confidence that mortgagees will pay back a loan with interest

Confidence that one can liquidate their position from a fund at a moment's notice if you need the cash

During the financial crisis of 2007 and 2008, real estate funds were likewise hit by redemptions and forced to halt withdrawals, contributing to a crash in property prices of more than 40 percent from their peak in the UK. Real Estate funds are not as liquid as equity or bond funds. Though these funds keep anywhere between 15-20% in cash to meet redemption pressure, any sharp increase would mean selling their assets to generate cash. However vulture buyers of these assets are also very astute. They tend to let the dust settle until they start to purchasing (at very distressed levels- to be further discussed)

If these tenants start to capitulate fear sets in and dominoes fall in rapid successions.

Bill Gross, the legendary fund manager at Janus Capital Group Inc stated;

"The system doesn't allow liquidity to flow into the proper places. If these property funds are just one indication, perhaps there will be others to follow. I think it's something to worry about."

These property funds are structured as open-end funds, which give the illusion to offer liquidity however as in 2007 and in present this is not the case. There is a fundamental mismatch between the open-ended design of the investment vehicle and the relative illiquidity of a significant portion of the assets it holds. In order to get your money back you sell your shares back to the fund manager, which under "normal" market conditions is not an issue. However and the big however is when everyone panics and heads for the exit at the same time, the cash cushion evaporates and those who did not react need the fund to sell some property to raise liquidity. Selling property at a decent price takes a while, especially if everyone else is selling at the same time. This puts funds in a tight corner!

While £18 billion of suspended assets is a relatively small number compared to other investments, it is an early indicator that panic has replaced confidence in UK property.

Adding fuel to the fire is that the sector is funded by a lot of debt, which increases the risk that other markets catch the financial contagion. If fire sales depress prices, then banks and other lenders exposed to the market could begin to take losses. And once confidence in banks has been shaken, it is hard to get back.

This brings us to our next fun topic

Do you Remember Northern Rock?

Northern Rock has the unique reputation for becoming the first British bank in 150 years to suffer a bank run after having had to approach the Bank of England for a loan facility. Northern Rock was not able to find a buyer and in 2008 the UK Government became the proud owner of Northern Rock.

When I look at the stock charts of the leading banks I am baffled as how they can keep on lending. Granted Mark Carney has now made a third statement since the referendum, he that will relax banking sector rules to free up lending to households and businesses. Carney has promised to release £150 billion. However, what I still don't seem to understand was earlier articles after the Brexit that something like £3 trillion were vaporized. What really is £150 billion for an economy the size of the UK?

Personally as this eBook is all about how to protect and grow assets, it is hard to feel very secure leaving money in the banks when their share prices are so low and we have insurance only up to £75,000 per account.

Or Even Worse- Deutsche Bank who is the proud owner of 70 something trillion of (toxic?) derivatives.

What confirmed my worries was a recent call from a doctor from London. He sent this email…

Please call me asap on 07894XXXXXX

Sent from my iPhone

My colleague called him and the doctor told him he had £300,000 sitting at his bank and was very concerned. Ok, there only has been one Northern Rock...but who knows he stated. The Doctor said the same thing we have said countless times. The properties in which we invest in the North West have been around for a 100 years and will be for another 100 years after we are gone. Wow....music to our ears. We are not the only ones who are skeptical of bonds, real estate funds, banks, new gorgeous luxury flats or stocks....

Bricks and Mortar....

Volatility of Stocks

Taking out the hype of buy and hold stocks but living the ups and downs. How many of us really enjoyed seeing the stock fall in 2007-2008. Ok, yes it came back. But what happens if you needed that money for some emergency. Lets dig a little deeper. What about the dot com bubble in the early 2000s. How many times can we stomach a deep draw down twice in a decade. If you like roller coasters be my guest.

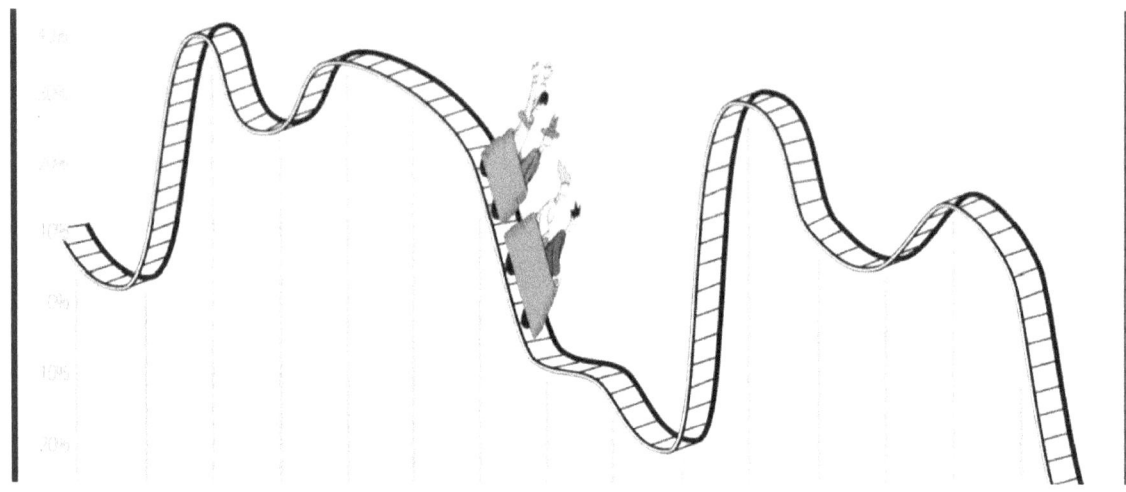

For those of us who are older, I am sure they remember the "misery" of 1973. That only took 12 years to get to the level before hand. For our grand parents who invested prior to the Great Depression that only took 25 years to come back to those levels prior. Honestly who could have waited????

Bond Funds & Interest returns

Should I start with the ridiculous levels of interest that banks pay or the risks investors are taking to get just a little more yield. All savers relying on interest are all are disappointed from the historic low levels of interest being paid by banks. However, I know so many so called smart investors who have bragged to me that they are making 4-5% a year "Safely?". They have invested in High Yield bonds.

A high-yield bond is a high paying bond with a lower credit rating than investment-grade corporate bonds, Treasury bonds and municipal bonds. Because of the higher risk of default, these bonds pay a higher yield than investment grade bonds. I have personally seen several cycles already of these so called safe bonds that the borrowers simply stop paying and the underlying collateral is not sufficient.

Is it really worth the risk?

Following the Brexit the contagion spread to the US High Yield market. **High-yield funds reported their second largest daily outflow on record of $-1.9 billion**, second only to $-2.7 billion the day after the Third Avenue fund closure. Meanwhile, the HY ex-commodity cash index initially widened 68bps, **or as much as it did in the first two days following Lehman bankruptcy.** It has since retraced some of these losses. Year-to-date, high yield spreads excluding commodity are 29 bps wider so far. Other leading indicators, such as implied volatility, AA spreads and financials all have increased signifying enhanced risk.

Is it really worth the risk?

So how do make our money work smarter for us???

Read on and I will share with you my own private strategies in which you can replicate for yourselves. Please realize they are only my personal opinions and my approach to investing. Ask your own financial investor for their thoughts.

When investing there are no sure things or guarantees!

Everything has risks.

I try to mitigate my risks however I can still lose money in my investments.

http://www.bhinvestment.co.uk/

My Investment Story

During University I began to take notice of and witnessed the investment manias and the delusions of the crowds and their hype. I witnessed what transpired to gold. This so-called bastion of stability fell nearly 70% from the 1980s through the early 2000s. Interest rates were running close to 18% and the stability of the financial system was questioned. I saw real estate giants' collapse and property prices crash. No one could believe how cheap property became. Property went from being the must have asset to investors throwing keys back to the banks. At a very young age I witnessed the carnage.

However fortunes could have been made by buying these properties at that time. Nothing changed as I was growing up. In other asset classes bubbles appeared and crashed. Stocks that everyone had to own—called the greatest investments in 2000—ended up imploding. I remember being instructed by a colleague that I should buy tech stocks before there were no stocks left. We all know what happened to the NASDAQ. The story sadly continued with real estate, an investment that also was considered safe.

Investing is risky. Bad things can happen and eventually do happen to all assets. There are no safe havens. Valuations get out of whack, industries change, managers screw up, politicians make terrible decisions, and things don't always work out as expected. In order to survive we must have the ability to ignore crowds and hype. In order to provide for our families we need to have a complete plan. The vast majority of investors spend less time planning their investment future than deciding what to eat for dinner. It is easier for them to buy whatever the so-called professionals feed us.

I had made our families money by a business which I started in college in the clothing business. I learned to buy cheap. I would buy seconds and slightly damaged clothing from manufacturers. I would buy below the market and sell value. I have used the same concepts in real estate. I sold the business in 1994 and sought out a way to make our money work for us. I avidly saved during the years I was making a lot of money. We enjoyed life, yet we lived below our means. We would buy luxury cars, but buy them used with 10,000 or less miles. It was very clear to me that saving was more important than investing. I had to have resources to invest with. I saw my peers who were more interested in having the latest gadgets and not saving for a rainy day or even investing. They would have been better off if they devoted that energy to figuring out how to save more money than live for the moment.

Most financial problems are caused by debt. I witnessed a colleague of mine, who I went to college with, who earned several hundred thousand dollars a year as a specialist in an advanced field. He declared bankruptcy in 2009 and will probably need to work well into his 70s.

There are people in my mother's condo who never made a lot of money throughout their lifetime, however they avoided debt, invested in real estate and are living a comfortable retirement. Actually I learned the most about real estate from my mother. She is still active in real estate. Last year she conveyed on a flat in her building and flipped for a 50% profit in 4 months start to finish.

Investing first started out as an interest. This interest grew into a passion, or as my wife would say at times—an obsession. Upon the sale of my business, I did not know what to do with the proceeds. I asked my accountant and my attorney for suggestions. I asked who their most successful client was. I was given a name, a phone number and was told he had made money for decades. He invested in beaten up real estate and would renovate the properties. Some of them he sold on in which he would offer to finance the investors or he simply rented them.

I started my real estate experience started by owning a bridging company in South Florida (Yes I am originally from the US). The bridging opened up many doors for me. I ended up entering a JV partnership with a builder in which we built affordable housing. We would build 9 houses at a time at all different stages. It was a complete cycle. As one was sold we would have another coming out of the ground. I ended branching out even more. I would renovate blocks of flats and even houses. Constantly turning over properties and compounding money. By 2006 I became very wary what was happening in the US real estate markets. I closed my bridging and stopped building. Thank GD I avoided one of the greatest turn downs in real estate in US History.

Experience Andrew Abraham

1. Owner of a bridging company based in Florida with turnover of $30,000,000 with 6 month interest only loans @12% interest to builders and renovators. I utilized family funds & 5 high net worth investors as JV partners. We had deep pockets to do deals consistently.

2. I formed a Minority business with a builder in which we regenerated inner city blighted areas. We obtained the land for free by the city in order to both improve neighborhoods and supply first time home buyers a quality dwelling. All we had to do was build, buyers were given grants and loans from local programs (ship program).

(Typical House I would build)

3. Purchased numerous parcels of land in Florida, Tennessee and North Carolina for single family housing. Packaged and sold off to Builders and developers.

4. Warehouse project of 13 acres of 100,000 sq ft. Tripled investment within 1 year each of us made over $1,000,000. Split the deal with a JV partner.

However I was not that smart to get in at the bottom. I moved overseas and by 2011 I looked at projects in the Czech Republic, Cyprus and Portugal. It was only there after I found the promised land of (Sunny) Manchester real estate. Prices were still below the 2007 peak. There was a shortage of housing. Even Tony Blair's wife was investing in Manchester. I chuckled that she must know something that I surely did not. The BBC built media city. Mostly it was cheap and property yields were fantastic compared to London.

I jumped over the pond and landed in Manchester!

JV Partners

Kramer Brothers

The Kramer brothers grew up in Manchester and have been involved in real estate since 1997. They own approximately 50 terraced houses in which they rent out. Great deal of experience in renovating housing and more importantly, managing the properties. Survived the 2008 property crash and going strong since.

Robert Jones & Chris Kershaw

- Robert Jones, Director. Robert has been investing in Property across the North West (UK) since 2005. Living in Manchester, he runs a property training and consulting company (www.propertyinvestmentsuk.co.uk) and alongside building his own property portfolio has been sourcing properties for UK based and worldwide investors since 2007.

- Chris Kershaw, Director. Chris purchased his first property investment in 2007 and has previously worked for Clear Channel as a Sales Account Manager across some of its larger B2B clients. Chris has been full time in property since early 2014 and now runs (www.quicksaleuk.co.uk) with Robert Jones and has been hands on sourcing deals for clients whilst growing his own portfolio.

http://www.bhinvestment.co.uk/

Why Manchester?

I have my opinions. My rational is rather simple. There are 3 million people living in Manchester. Brexit or not, there is a housing shortage. Prices are just now recovering from 2008 crash levels. Block brick housing some of which are 100 years old. There exists an extreme shortage and need of housing for social housing. The UK Government and local governments are willing to assist in renovation costs and enter into long term agreements.

Prices in Manchester stand the chance of major appreciation in the near term due to the new High Speed train to London. HS2 will reduce the average journey time from central Manchester to central London from 2 hours 8 minutes to 1 hour 8. This new train will make Manchester a bedroom commuter community of London.

The property experts have their opinions and even one can do a simple Google search and find even more reasons for Manchester.

This article I found from Select Property :

UK real estate growth is currently strongest in regional markets, with Manchester leading the way. So what's making the north-west a key investor hotspot?

For international investors, buying property in the UK has traditionally meant buying property in London.

The sustained growth of the capital's prime real estate made it the logical investment location. The average property price in London in January 1995 was £126,295. By June 2015, this had risen to £611,340 in June 2015, representing a 384% return on investment.

Now, however, things have changed.

UK property assets have appreciated by 10% in the last 12 months. Yet it has been regional cities that have contributed most to this growth, with London's house price inflation standing at just 5.2%.

Nowhere has this regional growth been felt more than in Manchester. Just this week Knight Frank reported that Manchester had seen commercial office investment sales in the third quarter of 2015 40% above the five-year quarterly average. Economic growth in the area, creating thousands of new jobs, means that businesses in the region desperately need new office spaces, prompting such high levels of investment.

It is performance that's being mirrored in all of the city's property sectors. So what's making Manchester the epicenter of regional UK real estate investment?

1. A city at the start of a growth curve

Investing in a market on the brink of huge growth has the potential to reap big rewards. Just ask an investor who bought in London twenty years ago.

This curve underlined just how important it is to notice emerging markets and acquire assets early. But London is now reaching the end of this cycle, with Knight Frank noticing a fall in interest for real estate in the city from key international investor communities.

All evidence points to Manchester enjoying a similar type of growth curve seen in London over the next few years. Sustained job growth is driving the large-scale investment in the city's commercial property sector – and these workers also need a place to live.

Manchester has been named by HSBC as the UK's number one city for property investment, boasting yield growth almost 13 times the pace of those in London in recent years.

Manchester has also enjoyed 18% capital growth in the last 18 months. With an outlook of sustained economic investment, a growing population and shrinking supply of property, prices are expected to grow by a further 22.2% in the next three years.

And this is just the start.

2. 7 billion reasons to invest

Manchester is one of the core cities at the heart of the UK government's Northern Powerhouse plans.

£7 billion worth of investment is planned for the region, as Britain attempts to rebalance the economic power of the country away from London. New devolved powers, high-speed rail links and enterprise zones with favorable tax conditions are just a few of the planned projects that will drive the economy of Manchester, bringing more visitors and creating new jobs.

Last month Chinese president Xi Jinping visited Manchester and announced a £4 million construction project kick started by Bejing Construction and Engineering Group (BCEG), as well as unveiling a new direct flight route from Beijing to Manchester with Hainan Airlines, which will begin service in 2016.

Such sustained economic investment will naturally impact on Manchester's real estate market.

3. A young population that needs a place to live

It's a city that people want to be part of. Manchester's population is rising at three times the national average, yet it's a city with one of the lowest levels of housing stock in the country.

What makes this imbalance more profound is the demographics of the population. Manchester is home to 60% more 25 to 29-year-olds than the rest of the UK. With changing attitudes towards homeownership in Britain and forecasts predicting that over 50% of 20 to 39-year-olds will be renting their property for 2025, Manchester's population is seen as a 'golden demographic' in the eyes of many investors.

Institutions have already been quick to identify this opportunity. Deloitte Real Estate state that 10,000 new private rented sector (PRS) units are due to be built in Manchester over the next few years, investment that's been predominantly driven by pension funds, insurance companies and private businesses

http://www.bhinvestment.co.uk/

Profiting the Brexit by Property Investing

Everyone has their opinions of what might happen with the Brexit. There are many of the camp full of despair and those that see opportunity on the horizon. Contrarily there those in the camp, that this was all a big bluff.

Shares in the UK's biggest companies are now worth more than they were before the vote. The world has not ended. Life seems to be carrying on more or less as normal, doesn't it? So was it all scaremongering? If you are inclined to think along these lines, to conclude that "the experts" all got it hopelessly wrong, think again.

The fact is that there has already been a significant shock to the financial markets. Some time in the near future unless you prepare Brexit will have a negative impact on people's living standards and economic opportunities. This is not necessarily immediately obvious to people.

The £ has shifted more, in an extremely faster pace than at any point since the major currencies of the world were allowed to float freely against each beginning in the early 1970s. Against the dollar, sterling is now at its weakest since 1986. This will cause inflation at some point.

There are those who look at the stock market and claim it is now higher than before the Brexit.

However is it?

The FTSE 250, which is made up of smaller companies that predominantly generate their revenues in the UK, is down around 10 per cent since the vote. This is a much better indication of financial traders' expectations of how the referendum result will ultimately affect UK companies' profits. Yes, exporters will benefit as well as there will be increased tourism from abroad but offsetting against the general economy is a much deeper question.

The Bank of England's Governor, Mark Carney, has stated the need for a short-term interest rate cut over the next two months to prop up domestic spending. That could mean a reduction in families' monthly mortgage interest payments. Good news right???

Not really if you a saver! If the Bank of England base rate is cut to a new historic low of 0.25 per cent, that would also imply another reduction in the interest paid on people's cash savings in banks. Bear in mind that elderly savers were already howling about their rock bottom savings returns.

People are being squeezed between a volatile stock market, non existent bond yielding market and uncertainty!

I see opportunity and want to help you to see the opportunities as well especially where I have decades of real time experience.

I strongly believe that in times of uncertainty and crisis wealth can be protected and even grow with the proper mindset, hard work and strict adherence to risk.

Over the majority of my life I have been investing in real estate. I have lived through various cycles and strongly believe if we get into a tough situation in the realm of real estate, fortunes can be created as they have in the past. However do not think for one second, this is a get rich quick. This is a work hard, you must continue to work hard through countless adversity, face all kinds of issues, work through all kinds of disappointments and simply never give up.

Now might be one of the best times for Britons to buy a home because property price growth is significantly slowing down. A perfect storm might be brewing with the toxic combination of stamp duty and the Brexit.

Stamp Duty Have Already Impacted House Pricing & Demand

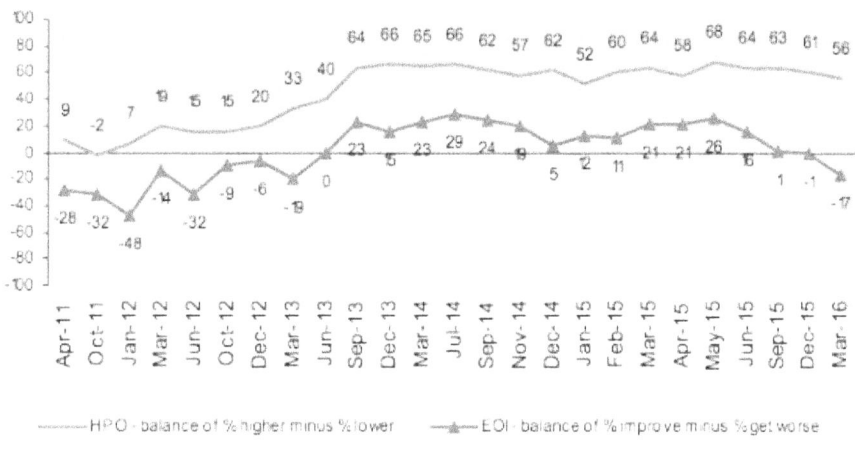

The Stamp Duty tax change in April this year has already helped contribute to fewer people buying properties and therefore putting a dampener on prices.

Stamp duty is a tax placed on buyers when they purchase a property in the UK. It is payable on completion of the property and under the new system, introduced in April, works out at an extra £93,750 if you're buying a property at £1.5 million, according to the government's stamp duty tax calculator. However, if you're buying a property for £5 million, you'll be forking out £513,750 just in stamp duty fees.

If you own more than one property, a 3% stamp duty is applied. This new fee also came into force in April and is applicable to buy-to-let investors and those who are buying a second home. This 3% fee is on top of the extra cost of a new purchase in April.

Halifax said this move has already killed off price growth, no matter how imbalanced the supply and demand equation is:

"Home sales stabilized in May. The introduction of higher stamp duty tax rates for buy to let and a second home in April has had a substantial impact on house sales in recent months. A rush to complete sales ahead of the tax change caused a sharp rise in March, which was followed by a substantial decline in April.

The stamp duty change has also affected mortgage approvals in recent months. The volume of mortgage approvals for house purchases – a leading indicator of completed house sales – increased by 1.3% between April and May. Nonetheless, approvals in the three months to May were 6% lower than in the preceding three months."

Martin Ellis, Halifax housing economist, states:

"There is evidence that the underlying pace of house growth may be easing. House prices in the three months to June were 1.2% higher than in the previous quarter; down from 1.5% in May. The annual rate of growth fell from 9.2% in May to 8.4%; the lowest since July 2015. House prices continue to increase, albeit at a slower rate, but this precedes the EU referendum result, therefore it is far too early to determine any impact since."

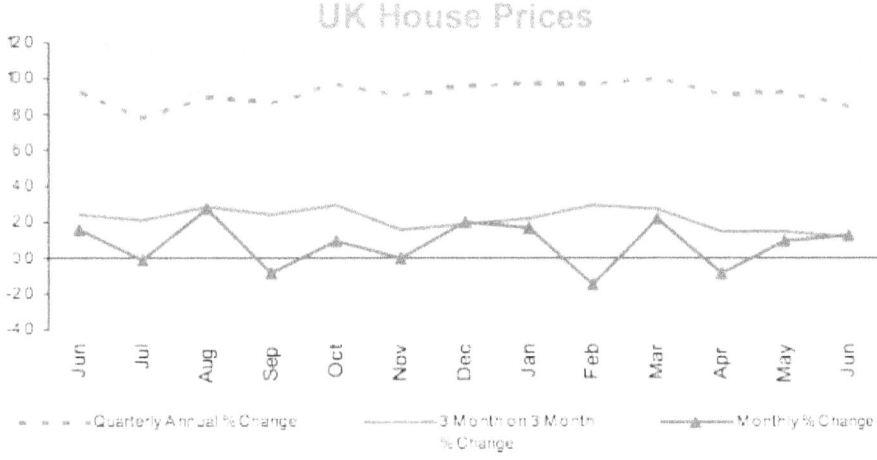

What Ellis from Halifax says is true — it is too early to determine the absolute effect of what Brexit will do to property prices. However, that uncertainty has also put a dampener on prices because it is causing more Brits to put home buying on pause, in case they need that cash in the event of an economic downturn, and foreign investors are holding off on hovering up investment buys until they know what is really going on.

The NACM also demonstrates the lessening of credit and bankruptcies are starting to surge!

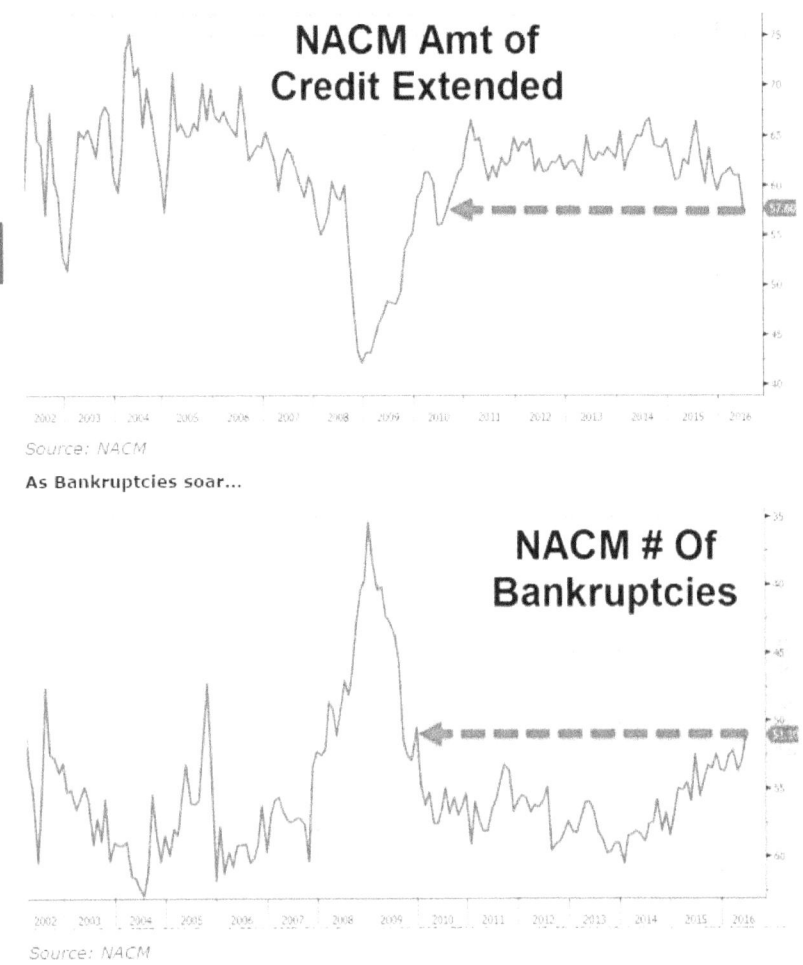

As Bankruptcies soar...

Property Investment Strategies- Brexit or Not

The following are time tested ideas of property investment strategies that I have used over the years. During uncertain times or recessionary times these ideas stand out. The key to making money is buying right and under leveraging. You will need to have money or access to money. There is always access to money even in the toughest times via joint ventures. This is not the time to go to the banks and sign personal guarantees and risk your future. In order to raise assets through Joint ventures you need to prove to that partner who can be a family member, friend or even acquaintance that you have knowledge and can make them money. Further one I will discuss in much greater depth the strategies in which I have used over the years. Regardless of how much money one might have, they never have enough.

My Personal Real Estate Approach

Buying Below Value- Anticipating the Real Estate Market can Even Weaken Further

1. Terraced Housing investment
2. Commercial to Residential (Making flats out of warehouses, pubs or offices)
3. Houses of Multiple Occupancy (HMO for short)

What I Completely Avoid

Pre- Construction Buildings

Let's face it; these modern buildings have more than a monetary appeal. They have an ascetic and architectural beauty. Bottom line is they are desirable and sexy.

Terraced housing on the surface of it is not as sexy as pre construction of lovely flats in the middle of the city.

I have personally seen countless investors burned by placing deposits on these lovely flats. In all reality what I have witnessed is they are really placing a bet that these flats will be finished and go up in value once they are finished. During the good times, many times this occurs. However when the cycle starts to change profits can easily evaporate and just losses mount very quickly.

When looking at the Manchester or London skyline, countless new projects are in process. Who was buying all of these projects & who can afford them; Investors from abroad such as Saudi Arabia or China?

Maybe?????

Investing in Terraced Housing

I like the boring terraced housing especially in the North West, more so Manchester. I like the yields in these properties versus the hope and prayer for massive price appreciation as in London in all areas from Terraced housing to HMOs and conversion projects. These yields have been solid; however in the world in which we live in, anything can happen.

I personally believe investing in Terraced houses in the North West with extremely low leverage with a capital repayment mortgage one can compound wealth. Do not think to be a gun slinger unlike those investors in the pre crash days use all of the banks money. These gunslingers are long gone and so are their portfolios. I know this against the grain of so many real estate investors today who want 70% plus LTV interest only variable loans. They pull out all their money and wash & rinse in the next property. Only problem is that they do not have liquidity for an eventual hiccup in the housing market. I promise you there will be a hiccup. It is as certain as the sun rising and sun setting every day.

I believe in the turtle approach as a pose to the hair. The hair is faster yet does not finish the race. Prior to the crash in 2008, some property investors had hundreds of properties. Sadly many have none left. Values can go up and down and in 2008 they went down to everyone's chagrin.

I believe to build up a portfolio slow and steady. Purchase below value and renovate the properties. Live a humble life and reinvest your profits into more houses. Start small and slow. Be consistent and hard working.

You can figure on average a gross yield of around 8%. I would suggest looking for working tenants as a pose to LHA & DSS. Be conservative with all of your expenses such as maintenance and voids. Most important is under leverage. In today's mortgage world some fantastic low rates are available. This debt can become an asset as at some point there will be an interest rate rise. I personally would only look for capital repayment and try to lock in as long as possible. The environment we are in now calls for being conservative. More so, I would look to buy 10-20% below the prices quoted before Brexit.

Real World Example of What is Possible with Terraced Houses

I want to share a real world example of what is achievable in real estate and particularly Manchester with hard work and patience.

Recently I met a gent who owns 150 homes in Manchester. He started 25 years ago. He purchased properties that no one wanted in Salford. Salford was a war zone back then. Today investors from Saudi Arabia to China are asking about investing in Salford.

These terraced properties today rent for £500 to £900 a month. Using the portal Rightmove.co.uk one can easily see the vast wealth created simply by buying simple terraced homes and keeping them. The values of the houses have increased over the years not even including all the rents accrued over the years.

11 Mere Avenue, Salford, Greater Manchester M6 5QW

£42,000	Terraced, Freehold	06 Oct 2004	2 bedrooms
£42,000	Terraced, Freehold	06 Oct 2004	
£28,000	Terraced, Freehold	26 Jul 2000	
£10,000	Terraced, Freehold	17 Mar 2000	

19 Mere Avenue, Salford, Greater Manchester M6 5QW

£72,000	Terraced, Freehold	08 Jul 2015	2 bedrooms
£71,950	Terraced, Freehold	03 Oct 2005	
£55,000	Terraced, Freehold	19 Apr 2005	
£19,950	Terraced, Freehold	13 Jul 2001	

3 Mere Avenue, Salford, Greater Manchester M6 5QW

£67,000	Terraced, Freehold	20 Dec 2007	3 bedrooms
£21,000	Terraced, Freehold	23 Feb 2001	
£9,000	Terraced, Freehold	04 Dec 2000	

Time for Cheeky offers?

In today's Brexit world, what I see happening is that smart investors are putting in low ball offers. We are doing the same and making cash offers 20% below the Brexit. We are on both sides of offers; we are making them and others are offering us as we sell properties in order to buy properties with no bank leveraging.

For example, we own and are selling a block of HMOs with an asking price of £725,000. It comprises 5 income producing HMOs of £ 65,500 and we sell at a NET 9% return. These are a very specific type of HMO in which we have entered a 5 year contract with a corporate PLC offering social housing.

As part of this lease there is no management, no voids and maintenance is covered up to 5,000 per annum. The only expense is insurance which is several hundred quid a year.

commercial property consultants

FOR SALE

Liverpool Road, Irlam   Liverpool Road, Cadishead   Old Road, Wigan

Stelfox Street, Eccles   Stanley Street, Atherton

5 Income Producing Residential Investments

- Let to a blue chip covenant on 5-year lease
- Rental Income of £65,500pa
- Tenant repairs covered up to £5,000pa on each property
- Reflecting a Net Initial Yield 9% yield

Had several offers, one starting with £400,000. Honestly that is below are cost of purchase and renovation. Nothing to get mad as the investor was just trying it out. Now we have other offers which are substantially higher. More so we are creative and have offered an investor that we would hold a first charge on the property. We offered 35% down payment @ 5% rate. Cash on cash this investor will make 16.7% on his money.

A little better than the bank- What do you think?

Regarding our buying, Yes we are being laughed off on some of our offers however we are still able to purchase. I bought one property on the Friday of Brexit. This property was the cheapest property in the entire area. It was a repossession and I re- negotiated the price as fear was ripe.

This particular terraced house would not be rented to a family rather we would convert it to a HMO (House of Multiple Occupancy) and lease it to a corporate entity on a guaranteed 5 year lease, with no voids; maintenance covered up to 5,000 per annum. We will generate cash on cash around a 15% return yearly. **Where can you find that in today's world?**

This property could easily be used as a family let. I would strongly suggest working tenants or families. We have worked in the LHA arena and found ourselves baby sitters to some degree. With family lets depending on area and price paid 8% is achievable in the Greater Manchester area. This is not including potential price appreciation long term.

According to JLL, we are looking at 20% price increases over the next 4-5 years.

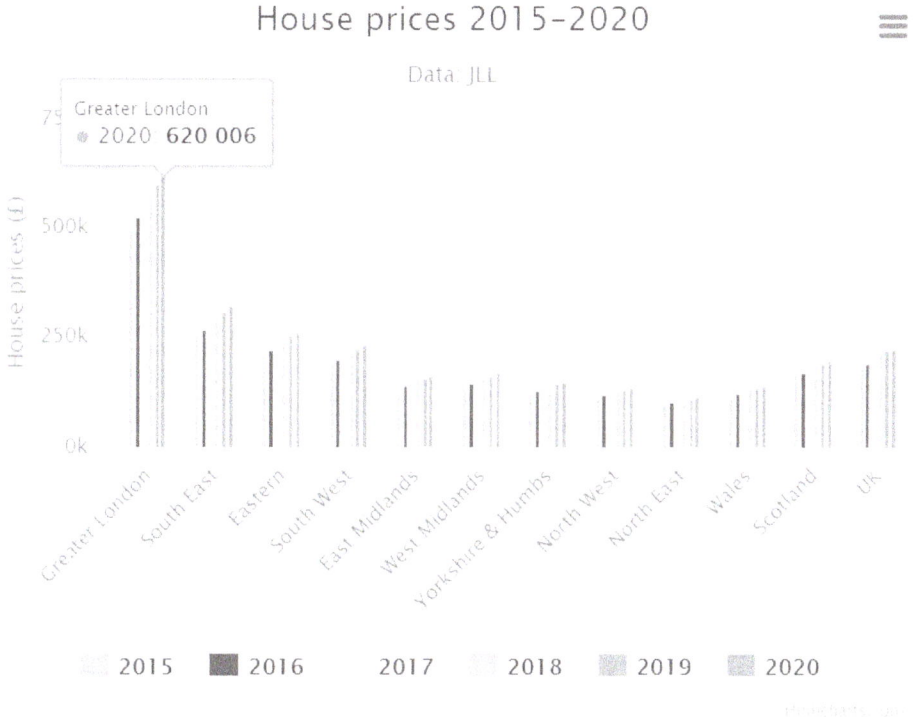

When you start including rent generated and appreciation 5 years or 10 years down the line, the numbers start becoming very interesting. Interesting is good, however there will be challenges from tenants who do not pay, tenants who do not respect the property and probably even more unknown issues. As I said before do not give up. Investing in real estate is a marathon!

http://www.bhinvestment.co.uk/

Crisis Investing From the Legendary Billionaires

In order to be a billionaire one must be different than the crowd. The crowd or herd seem to do all the same thing at the wrong times. How many of you remember April 2016 when every so call Buy to Let investor rushed to purchase property before the stamp duty increase?

Was this a sign of a top for real estate in the UK?

Only in hindsight will we really know.

Some of the worlds richest people made their money in the toughest times in all types of fields including real estate. The rational is very simple, during a crisis, assets can be mispriced due to forced liquidation by heavily indebted investors or quite simply FEAR!

Carlos Slim became one of the richest men in the world during the harsh recession in Mexico in the 1980s. He has a net worth of approx $50 Billion dollars. Slim built his diverse portfolio of businesses from a vast group of industries in one of the toughest economic periods in Mexico. His Grupo Carso owns companies in the fields of telecommunications, education, health care, industrial manufacturing, food and beverages, real estate, airlines, media, energy, hospitality, entertainment, technology, retail, sports and financial services. He bought when others were forced to liquidate.

We all know that Warren Buffett is one of the most successful investors of all time. We all know that Buffett is a value investor. He has sought out the best deals. In some many cases through out his career he has bought when others sought the shelter of the sidelines.

As Warren Buffett states

In the business world, the rearview mirror is always clearer than the windshield.

I am confident you have heard this statement of his

We simply attempt to be fearful when others are greedy and to be greedy only when others are fearful.

Bearing that in mind why can't you be a little like Warren Buffett?

Another of my favorite Buffett quotes is:

"It's better to hang out with people better than you.

Pick out associates whose behavior is better than yours and you'll drift in that direction." If you're reading about other successful investors, and surrounding yourself with those with more experience, then you'll be improving your chances all the time.

Another Buffett classic is:

"Someone's sitting in the shade today because someone planted a tree a long time ago."

The best time to grow your property portfolio was decades ago or maybe it would be even better if your grandparents had done it and passed that legacy down to you. If you're not in that position, if you perhaps have one or two properties or maybe if you don't even have any, my advice is to take action. And Warren also says:

"Opportunities come infrequently. When it rains gold, put out the bucket, not the thimble"

We're in a period of post referendum transition right now, and if you can't see the opportunity right now, it's time to align yourself with those people who can.

He was not born with a silver spoon in his mouth. He worked hard and he did the opposite of the masses.

Sam Zell – The Grave Dancer

Another legendary billionaire is Sam Zell - so wonderfully named the Grave Dancer. Zell started his career whilst he was in university. He managed a 15 unit apartment building in return for free room-and-board. Robert H. Lurie was a University friend of Zell and the pair started working together. They worked diligently and through hard work & by knowledge of what students wanted they gained the trust of the owner of a large block of flat. By the time they graduated university the pair were managing over 4,000 flats and owned hundreds of flats themselves.

Over the years Zell kept on making money in real estate as well as other industries. He even authored a kind of cook book of how exactly how to create wealth.

Sam Zell's Guide to Getting Really, Really Rich

1. Look for bargains, typically assets that are out of favor, in bankruptcy or otherwise distressed.
2. Ensure that those assets are of a high intrinsic quality.
3. Structure the deal so that you pay as little in taxes as legally possible.

These two gents are just two examples of value investors. There are countless. I remember my grandfather always speaking about the "Old Man on the Hill" Ditmeyer. This gent in the midst of the Great Depression was buying up everything from stocks to real estate. He was not leveraged and held on through the tough times. He built up wonderful cash flow and sold some of the distressed assets when times finally improved.

What is my point, very clearly we do not want to sink into despair. We must always remain strong and optimistic. The greatest opportunities are in the toughest of economic periods

Make Lemonade out of Lemons!!

Earlier, I stated the only certainty is uncertainty. Maybe the entire Brexit episode might subside and the world will be wonderful & maybe not. I do not have a crystal ball, but I do know that if I buy assets that are below market value & create value I will generate wealth. My world is real estate. My passion is real estate.

http://www.bhinvestment.co.uk/

Increasing your Profits via HMOs

It is never a bad thing to make increased profits for almost the same amount of work and investment. Houses of Multiple Occupancy are just the ticket. HMOs are rather encompassing. The general concept is that unrelated people are living in a shared accommodation. It is advantageous for tenants as well as landlords. Tenants can reside in nice areas, have full ammenties such as internet and all bills included & landlords can make greater profits.

Landlords can rent a whole house or you can virtually split it up like a pie and create a much greater income stream.

Some HMOs need to be licensed and some do not need to be.

We seek to create HMOs that do not fit the criteria set out by the home office thus we are not regulated. We convert large houses into HMOs in order to generate greater profits for ourselves and to the investors we work with.

You must have a licence if you're renting out a large HMO. Your property is defined as a large HMO if all of the following apply: it's rented to 5 or more people who form more than 1 household. it's at least 3 storeys high. tenants share toilet, bathroom or kitchen facilities. Jun 9, 2016
House in multiple occupation licence - GOV.UK

https://www.gov.uk/house-in-multiple-occupation-licence

The reason we focus on HMOs is that are more profits from a HMO rather a single let terraced house.

This is why we focus on these!

There are various versions however in very plain layman's terms, we rent rooms with shared kitchens and sometimes with shared or en-suite bathrooms. Primarily what we have done is taken a large house put in all the fire regulations such as interlink alarms and other HMO council regulations and transformed them into almost hotel like standards.

HMOs can be used for students, LHA tenants, social housing and working tenants.

Over the last 2 years we have purchased, refurbished, tenanted and sold approximately 35 HMOs to investors and crowd funding sites.

We even have a more profitable niche of HMOS by working in the Social Housing Field

We create, keep some and sell some of these Social Housing HMO properties to investors at approximately a 8 1/2% to 9% NET yield. Since we enter into long term contracts via the contract holder for the North West, there is no management...no voids and maintenance is covered up to a certain amount per year.

Some of the Social HMOs we keep ourselves and use the philosophy buy to sell in order to mitigate leverage.

Furthermore to create a very specific nice we have mostly have focused on HMOs which are for Social tenants. There can be many reasons in today's society that people and families need housing. The Home office steps in and takes care of these people.

We work with a major PLC who has a contract with the Home office to supply housing to those members of society who are in need.

This contract is one of the best ways I have ever seen in my career as an avenue to invest.

The contract itself runs for a 5 year period. There is a break clause for both parties but there is a severe shortage for social housing and even a back log. In the greater Manchester area due to this back log the PLC houses people in hotels at a cost of over £ 1,000,000 per month. The program has been in existence for over 20 years. There is no management, no voids and maintenance is covered up to £5,000 per year. All of these issues make it so much easier for us as landlords. It is extremely profitable as business people as well as we are helping society. What else can you ask for?

Over the last 2 years we have been both building our personal portfolios and selling these properties to investors from the Middle East as well as UK & crowd funding sites.

We sell these properties at a NET Return Yield to investors between 8 1/2 percent and up to 9 1/2 to an investment company who has buys numerous properties from us.

HCP165

£123,000 raised

9.5% gross yield. With a 5-year lease in place with a blue chip tenant, the property will be an income producing asset from legal completion, scheduled for 20th May. The tenant is responsible for...

Total Investment Required:	£123,000
Price Per Share:	£1000
Minimum Investment:	£1000
Minimum Term:	3 years

Funding (100%)

Read More

This is extremely unique as this is a net number. There is no management...no voids...and maintenance is covered up to 5,000 per year.

(Yes, we can sell these HMOs to you as well if you are interested)

Since this model is so extremely profitable & as well as the good it does to society we are in discussions for a JV situation with a group of Private Equity groups in London.

We are confident we can supply 100 HMOs per year with a current yield of 9% at a minimum. If they leverage that even 50% the yields grow dramatically. This will be a win win for us, the Private Equity fund, their investors and most importantly the tenants.

We are still in discussions with them as they are still waiting to see the fall out of the Brexit, however things are progressing.

Liverpool Road HMO Social Housing Example

Liverpool Road is located in Irlam a part of Salford in Manchester. It is an ideal location as it is within close walking distance to the train station into the center city of Manchester. My colleagues were originally scheduled to keep this for themselves however we jointly decided to put in the pot and sell on.

Actually this is one of the best deals we have done to date from a profitability standpoint. Only due to the hard work of my local partners and their relentless viewings and making offers were they able to find this deal.

Finding profitable deals is hard work!!!

BHAAA1836 Property Investments Ltd in account with JMW Solicitors LLP
p/o XXX Liverpool Road Irlam M44 5AD

COMPLETION TBC	PAYMENTS	RECEIPTS
PURCHASE PRICE	73,000.00	
ADD		
STAMP DUTY LAND TAX	NIL	
BILL OF COSTS PURCHASE	450.00	
VAT THEREON	90.00	
SDLT RETURN FEE	75.00	
VAT THEREON	15.00	
BANK CHARGE	30.00	
VAT THEREON	6.00	
COMPANY SEARCHES	4.00	
HM LAND REGISTRY SEARCHES	3.00	
HMLR REGISTRATION FEE	20.00	
SEARCH FEES	250.00	
ENVIRONMENTAL POLICY	68.00	
TOTAL PAYMENTS:	**74,011.00**	
LESS		
FUNDS RECEIVED FROM YOU		300.00
TOTAL RECEIPTS		**300.00**
BALANCE DUE FROM YOU TO COMPLETE		**73,711.00**

CLIENT ACCOUNT DETAILS FOR FUNDS TRANSFER:

Liverpool Rd is a 5 bedroom property paying per bedroom 57.50 per week or 14,950 per year.

Refurbishment cost approx 10,000

Total Cost 84,000 approx

17.7% cash on cash return

Where can you achieve those returns in today's world

Below are the final pictures

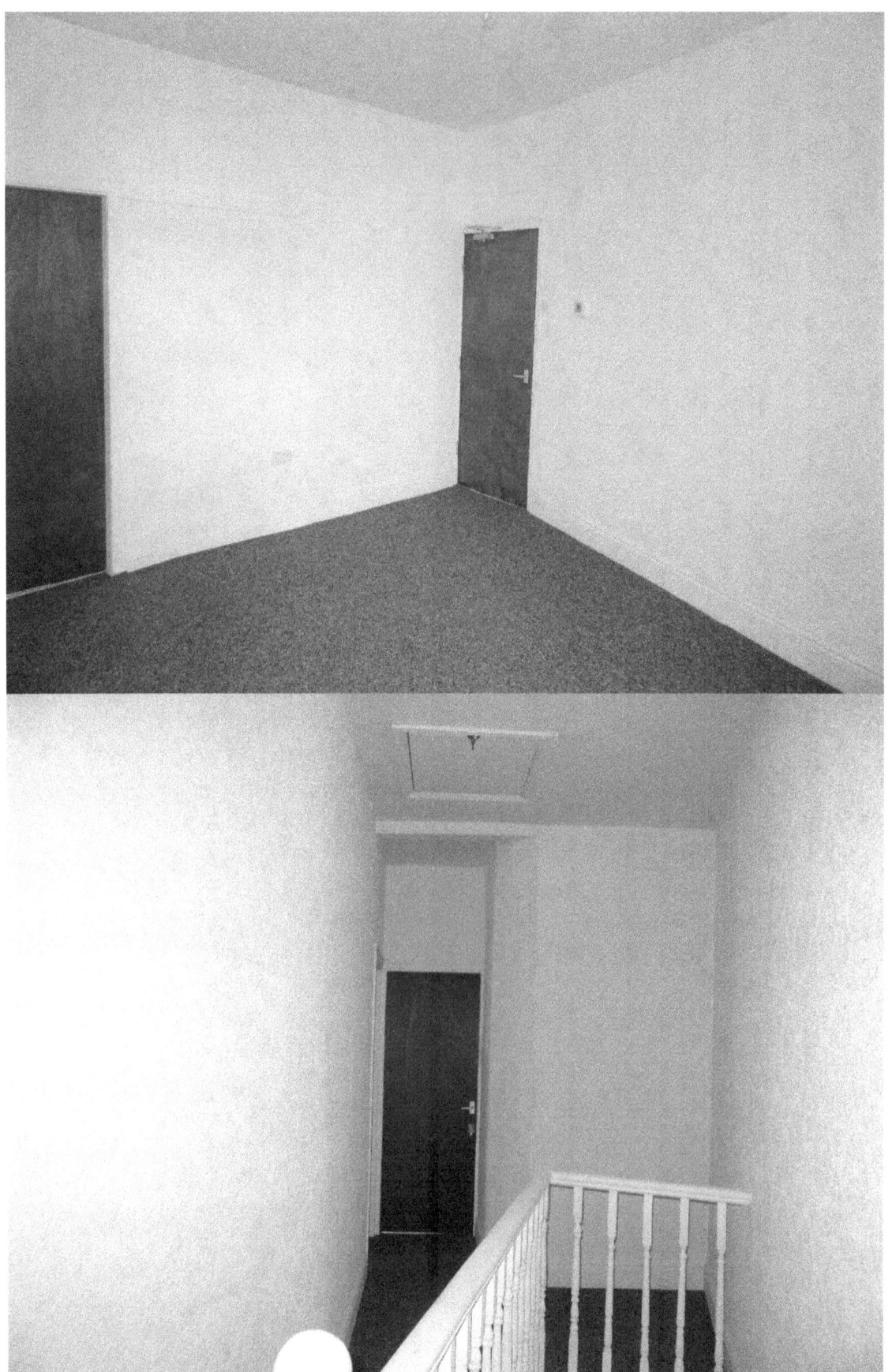

These are pictures of Before Refurbishment

Langton Street Salford Social Housing HMO

This was one of our earlier deals testing the waters with the PLC. We heard good things regarding the PLC however we did our due diligence (My wife tells me, I am obsessive compulsive paranoid). I always look at the worst case scenario and not the best. I knew we purchased the property below market value. I was concerned the property would pass all of their inspections and mostly that we would get paid timely. We had worked with a council and it seemed virtually every payment was wrong. This took time and energy to straighten out. I do not think it was intentional but rather they had a lot of properties and possibly not the right staff.

Purchase

Completion Statement
Relating to the Purchase of Langton Street, Seedley

Date: 23rd October 2014
Ref: 1755.05/PO/BHAAA

Monies Received

Funds on account from you	£0.00
Balance purchase funds from you	£0.00
Total Monies Received	**£0.00**

Monies Paid Out

Purchase Price of Property	£55,000.00
Local Authority, Drainage, Environmental and Coal Authority searches	£250.00
HMLR fee for pre-completion title searches	£3.00
HMLR fee for bankruptcy search	£0.00
HMLR fee for registration of transfer and charge	£20.00
Premium for chancel repair liability title indemnity insurance	£175.00
Redbird Conveyancing Limited Costs VAT and Disbursements	£636.00
Stamp Duty Land Tax	£0.00
Other Disbursements	£0.00
Total Monies Paid Out	**£56,084.00**

Sale

Completion Statement
Relating to the Sale of ● Langton Street

Date: 27th July 2015
Ref :   1755.14/PO/BHAAA

Monies Received

Sale Price of 1 Langton Street	£99,000.00
Apportionment for rent through 27th July 2015	£754.26
Total Monies Received	**£99,754.26**

Monies Paid Out

HMLR fee for office copies and title plan	£6.00
HMLR fee for 1899 copy conveyance	£25.00
Redbird Conveyancing Limited Costs VAT and Disbursements	£606.00
Total Monies Paid Out	**£637.00**
Balance Due To You	**£99,117.26**

E & OE

We made very nice profit in this property plus we collected rent until we sold it. Renovation costs range between 8,000 on some properties upwards to those we need to take back to the brick 15,000.

What is really amazing and what one of my JV partners told me, was that we would regret selling this property as it would only go up in value. He was spot on as the Gent we sold it to from Saudi Arabia sold it about a year later for much more. He collected rents and sold at an amazing profit. I have to add this is not just a gent from Saudi Arabia. He has a PHD in finance and is extremely smart. He saw value and he saw profit. This is someone who invests in all types of asset classes.

Using Rightmove.co.uk one can verify what I am stating....We made this property into a 4 Bedroom and we sold it to this investor at 8 1/2% yield.

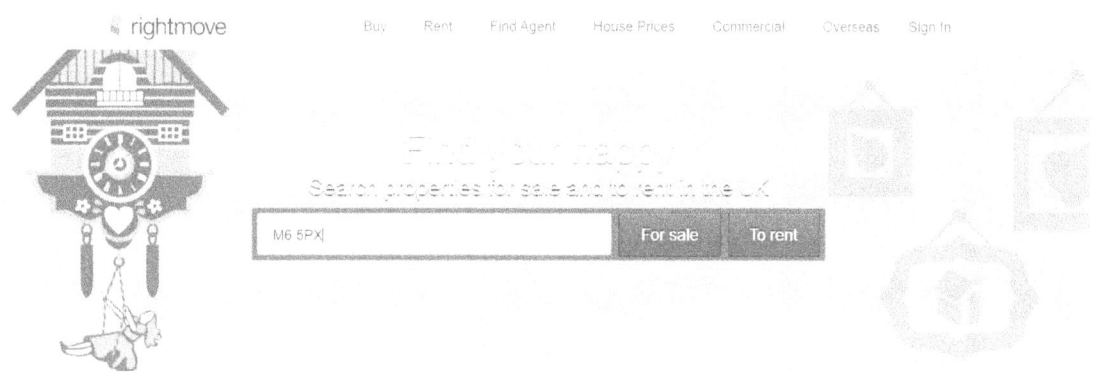

What is interesting the prices below are only for 2 and 3 bedrooms. A fourth bedroom makes the property even more valuable.

39 Laburnum Street, Salford, Greater Manchester M6 5LZ

| £121,000 | Terraced, Leasehold | 23 Oct 2015 | 2 bedrooms |
| £116,000 | Terraced, Leasehold | 08 Feb 2008 | |

186 Derby Road, Salford, Greater Manchester M5 5NA

| £141,000 | Terraced, Freehold | 25 Jan 2016 | 3 bedrooms |
| £141,000 | Terraced, Freehold | 25 Jan 2016 | |

9 Laburnum Street, Salford, Greater Manchester M6 5LZ

| £123,000 | Terraced, Leasehold | 27 Nov 2015 | 2 bedrooms |
| £134,000 | Terraced, Leasehold | 23 Nov 2007 | |

I am not exactly sure how much this investor sold the property for however would assume somewhere between 120,000 to 140,000. Additionally he collected at least 1 years worth of rent. All he had to do was sit and collect his BACS payments every month. There was no management....There was no void periods nor was there any maintenance.

Not a bad armchair investment? Maybe you want one?

Before pictures (fasten your seat belts) I am sure you would like to move in this condition???

Creating profits in real estate revolves around creating value. We are not afraid to get our hands dirty. We love hard work and mostly love the satisfaction of a property we are proud of and in our case serving society by providing housing to needy people.

After Pictures

Not Every Deal is a Home Run

Our goal is to keep on moving at all times. Not every deal is a home run. However doing 35 deals you can simply do the math and figure how profitable this can be (**Plus we invite you to join us by purchasing our properties or speak with us if you are interested in working with us under a JV agreement- more to follow**).

Every town has better parts and lesser parts. The same can be stated even on the same streets. All of the Social Housing HMOs go through all kinds of inspections and checks from the police to the councils. This re assures us that we are buying quality properties and hopefully they will increase in value (All types of experts have conservatively quoted at least 2-3% per annum in Greater Manchester)

Latest Property Market Trends in Manchester

- UK house prices increased by 0.2% in May
- Annualised house price growth across the UK slowed slightly to 4.7% in May
- Greater Manchester area sees 4.4% increase in values year on year
- Manchester house prices increase by 7.4% over the past year
- Salford sees 0.3% increase in values over the last month and 4.8% increase in values year-on-year
- Number of homes for sale remains at lowest levels since late 1970's

*Datasource: Nationwide House Price Index: End May 2016 and

Region	Monthly % Change	Annual % Change	Average Price £
Salford	0.3	4.8	£100,770
Manchester	1.2	7.4	£105,885
Greater Manchester	0.4	4.4	£113,292
North West	-0.1	5.3	£116,018

A suburb of Manchester is Wigan. Springfield in Wigan is a growth area and an area in which their is strong pride in ownership. We have completed on many deals in Wigan. Gidlow which is a main street not all that far from the city center was one of our first projects in Wigan.

Purchase Statement

Relating to the Purchase of XX Gidlow Lane

Date: 8th September 2015
Ref : 1755.24/PO/PIBL

Monies Received

Funds on account from you	£250.00
Balance purchase funds from you	£0.00

Total Monies Received — **£250.00**

Monies Paid Out

Purchase Price of Property	£85,000.00
Local Authority, Drainage, Environmental and Coal Authority searches	£210.33
Fee for replacement FENSA certificate	£40.00
HMLR fee for SIM search, office copies and title plans (x2)	£15.00
HMLR fee for pre-completion title searches	£3.00
HMLR fee for bankruptcy search	£0.00
HMLR fee for registration of transfer and charge	£40.00
Premium for chancel repair liability title indemnity insurance	£43.10
Redbird Conveyancing Limited Costs VAT and Disbursements	£666.00
Stamp Duty Land Tax	£0.00
Other Disbursements	£0.00

Total Monies Paid Out — **£86,017.43**

Balance Required to Complete — **£85,767.43**

Gidlow Sale

Completion Statement
Relating to the Sale of ● Gidlow Lane

Date: 17th November 2015
Ref: 1755.32/PO/PIBL

Monies Received

Sale Price of ● Gidlow Lane	£120,000.00
ADD apportionment for rent	£1,025.64
Total Monies Received	**£121,025.64**

Monies Paid Out

HMLR fee for office copies and title plan	£6.00
Premium for title indemnity policy for good leasehold title	£33.00
Premium for title indemnity policy for absence of easements	£105.00
Premium for title indemnity policy for lack of building regulation consent	£32.00
Redbird Conveyancing Limited Costs VAT and Disbursements	£606.00
Total Monies Paid Out	**£782.00**
Balance Due To You	**£120,243.64**

E & OE

What also is very interesting is the speed of the renovation of the property and sale. More so, it is very important to keep renovation costs in line. We know what everything should cost and we will only work with builders we have confidence in. Our builder worked diligently and Gidlow was held for a very short period. Velocity of sales are what make profits.

Renovation Pictures

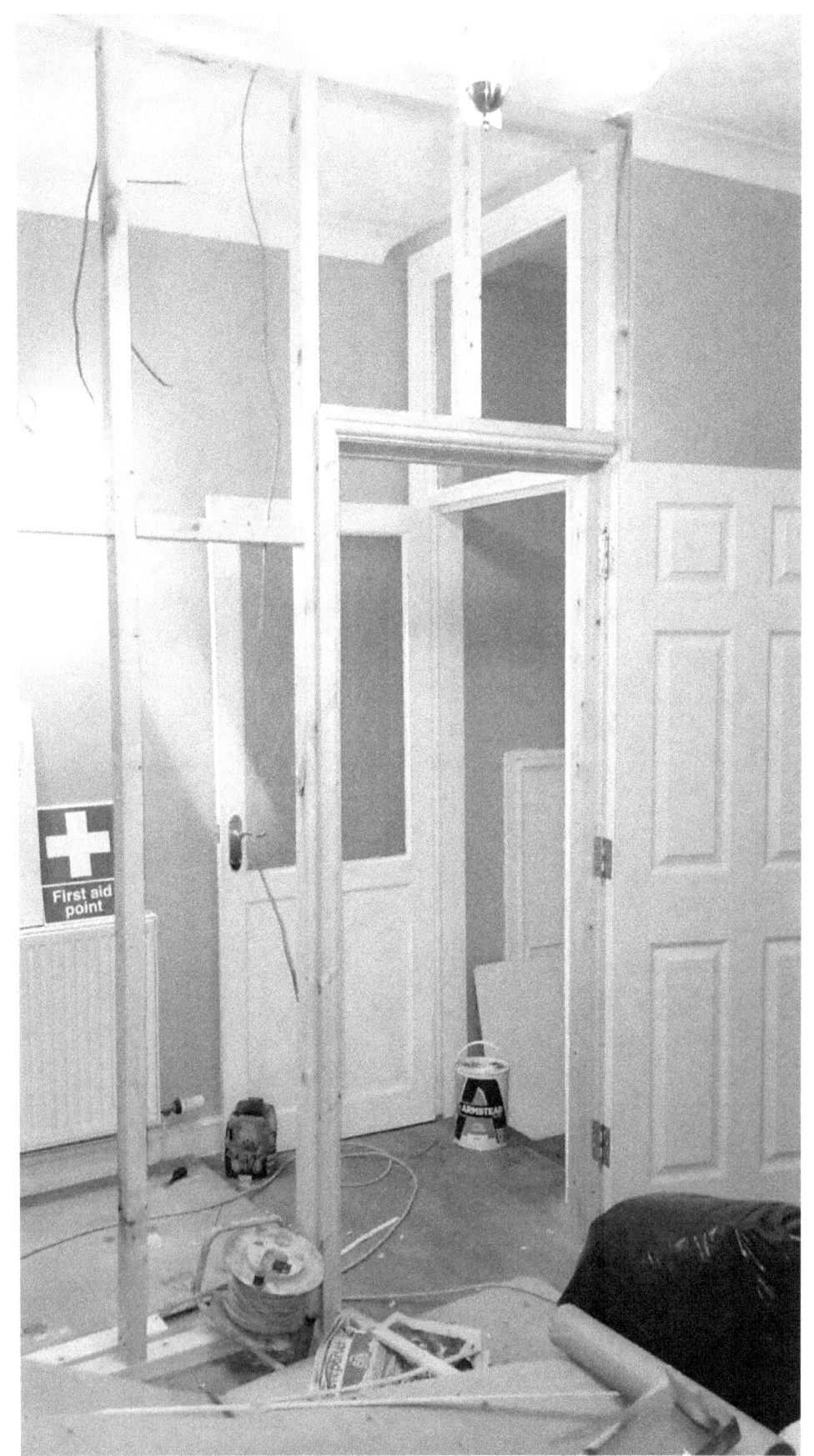

Final Pictures

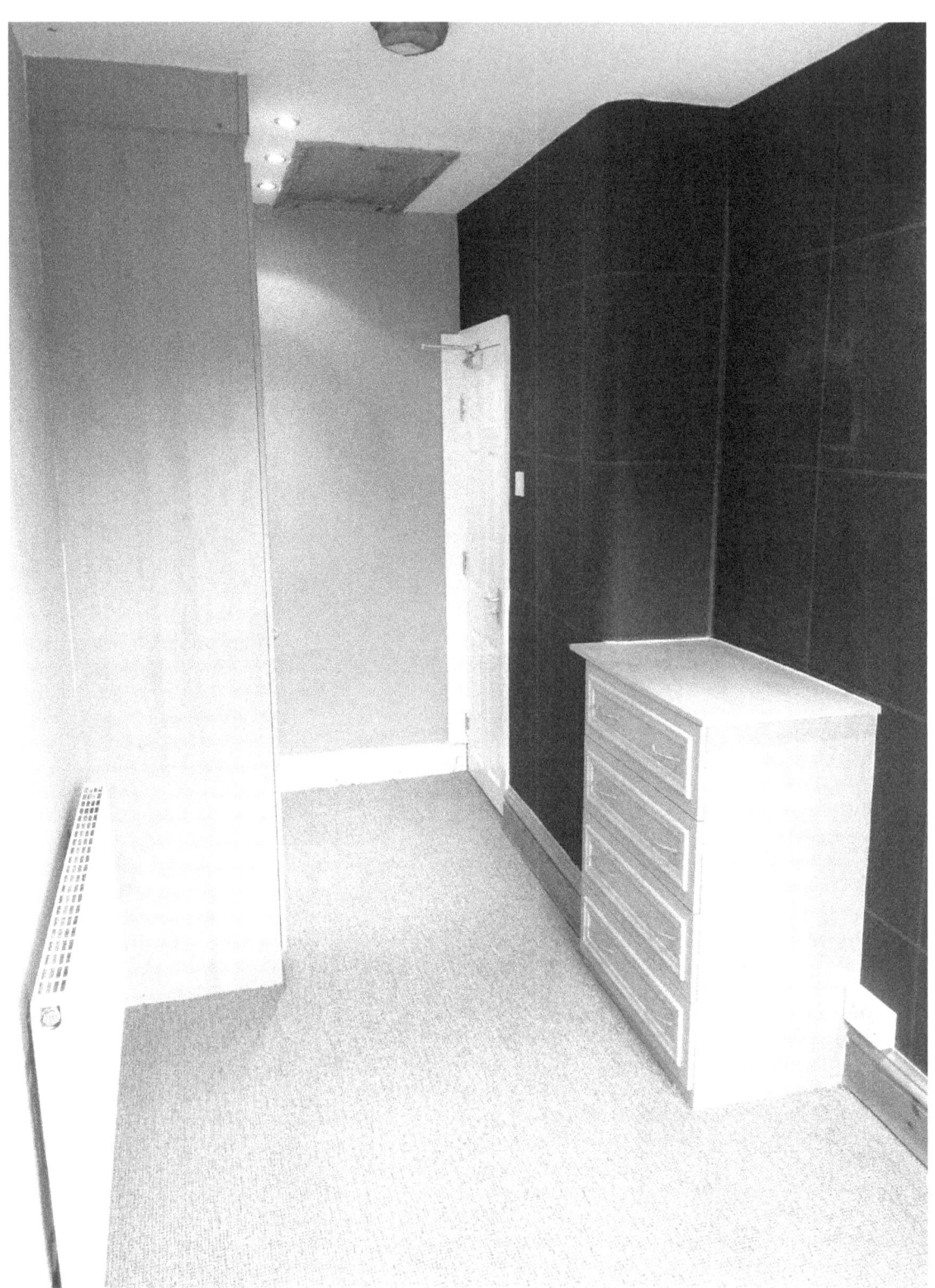

Watson Street, Salford Social Housing HMO Project

People from all over the world are looking at Salford properties. Maybe due to Media City & the BBC or simply the growth of Manchester. We have had enquiries from Hong Kong, Shanghai, Dubai, Israel and Saudi Arabia.

The Salford property is an easy hop to City center as well as Media City.

This property was renovated and turned into a Social Housing HMO. We sold it at a 9% net yield. This property generates £11,960.

Purchase Statement

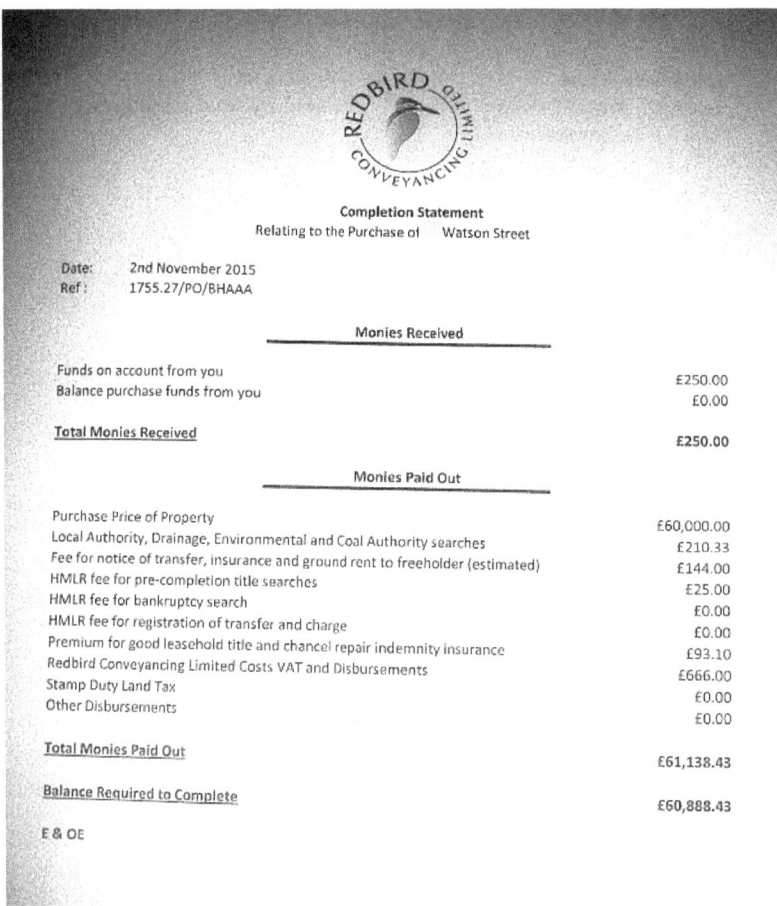

As you can note we purchased this property way below the market. Albeit it needed work, we created value by the renovation and the 5 year contract with the PLC.

The investor who purchased this property now is making 9% on his money net over the next 5 years.

A little bit better than the bank!!!

Sale Price

Completion Statement

Relating to the Sale of Watson Street Eccles

Date: Thursday, March 31, 2016
Ref: 1755.44/PO

Monies Received

Sale Price of 46 Caroline Street Irlam	£126,666.00
Rent Apportionment for period 1 March to 31 March 2016 (to be held to order)	£953.25
Total Monies Received	**£126,666.00**

Monies Paid Out

Estate Agents Fee - W T Gunson	£2,279.98
HMLR fee for office copies and title plan	£12.00
Redbird Conveyancing Limited Costs VAT and Disbursements	£702.00
Total Monies Paid Out	**£2,993.98**
Balance Due To You	**£123,672.02**

E & OE

Pictures during Renovation

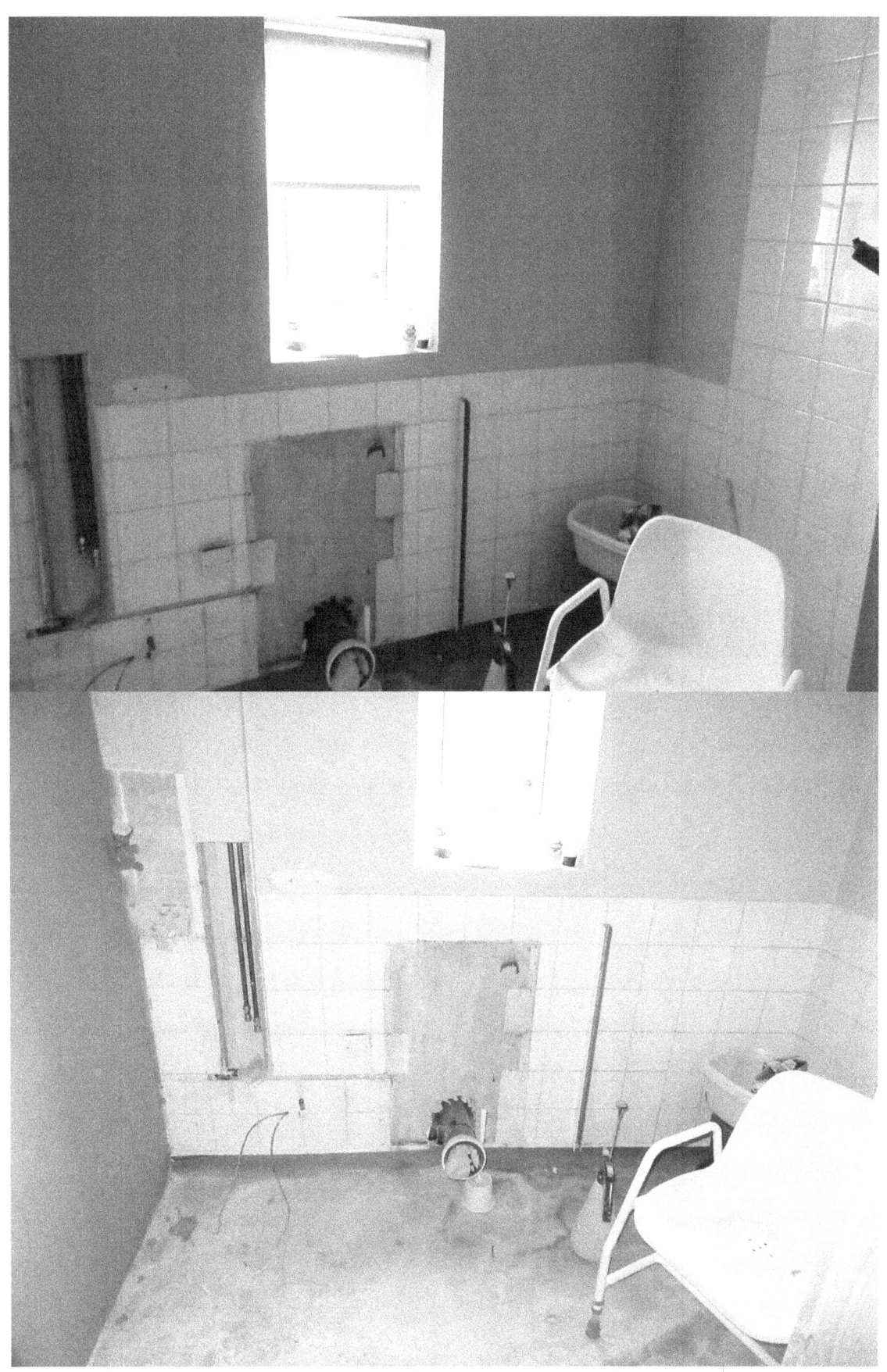

Professional Tenanted HMO Concepts

Professionals who move into our HMOs have it all. They have their council tax included. High speed internet is in all properties and room rates include electricity and all utilities. We do up the HMOs to a very high standard. We are not looking to squeeze our tenants. We want them to stay as long as possible. The higher the standard we make the HMO the less maintenance we will have as well. Some of the properties are en suite in which the tenants have their own private bathroom facilities and some have shared bathroom facilities. We get a higher rate on the private bathroom facilities. Both properties after being stabilized are high profit investments.

The tenants can range from those who just finished their studies and want to keep their expenses down yet live in nice areas to workers at Tesco & ASDA.

Both males and females live in the professional HMO properties. Rooms range from £80 per week up £125 per week.

(Following pictures are from a HMO my colleagues have completed and some are only demonstrative of how others have decorated rooms)

HMOs for working tenants are Ikea styled that are fresh and lively. We can have everything from someone just moving into to town to young professionals that can move in very easily with just a tooth brush. All bills are included from council tax, internet, cable, netflix and electric.

The financial numbers of a HMOs is in this example

4 Bed Terraced House in Manchester

This house was originally listed at £100,000. It was reduced £95,000. The property was viewed and a cash offer of £ 75,000 was placed. This offer was rejected and a best and final offer of £80,000. This property could support 4

en-suites which could rent in the area of £100 per week considering the standard in which we do these properties.

The property would need to significantly updated and renovated as it is tired and completely drab. A basic estimation is £10,000 per room. We have 4 rooms thus we would invest approx 40,000 subject to surprise expenses.

Cost 80,000
Stamp duty 2,300
Legal 1,000
Rehab 40,000
Cost subject to no major surprises 123,300

Even though we have inspections on properties, we allow 20% additional for refurbishment.

Gross Rentals based on full occupancy
20,800

16.9% Gross Rental Yield....

En-suites are like mini suites and usually rent very quickly and stay rented.

Less cost of council tax, utilities, voids, internet etc 30%

Net Rental Yields
16,000

Net Rental Yield
12.97 %

Refurbishment before

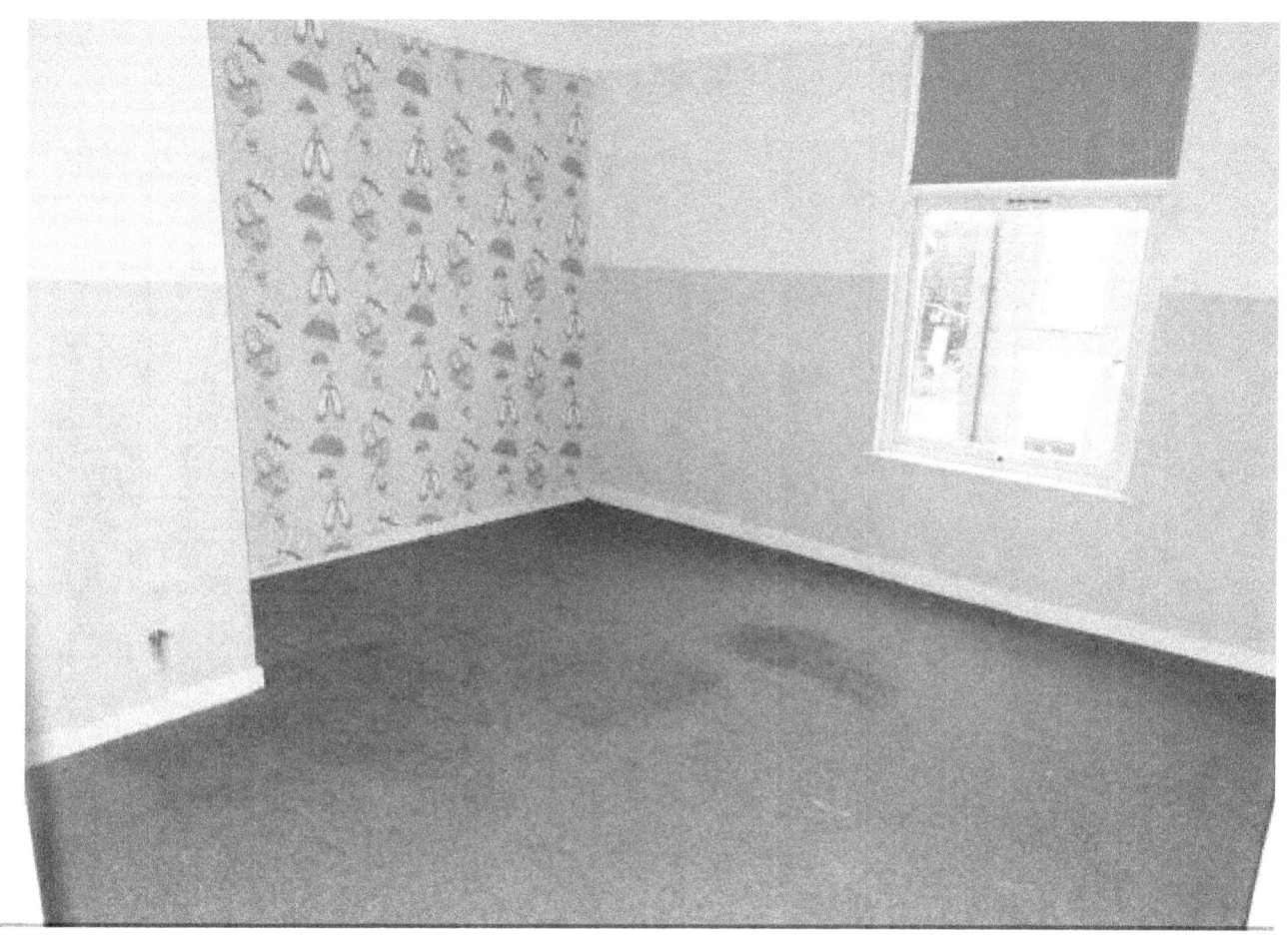

Would you like to live in the above or would you like to live in this?

Another example is Elizabeth Street in Pendlebury Manchester

This property will be a 5 bed with 2 en suites & 2 bathrooms. As the tenants will be sharing bathroom facilities the rent is much cheaper. We are looking at £80 per week. On the en-suite we could be pushing close to £ 100 per week. We will do this property up to the same standard as in the above pictures. This property will probably be the nicest property for rent in the area and should rent very quickly.

Currently the property is drab with magnolia walls yet clean. We will give it life with the Ikea finish...Bright and lively

The numbers on this one are as follows:

Purchase 74,000
Stamp duty 2,100
legal 1,000
Anticipated refurbishment 30,000-35,000

Total cost 112,000 (without any surprises)

3 Beds @ 80 per week= 12,480
2 en-suite @100 per week=10,400
=22,880

Gross return 20.4% in Salford.....Rather amazing

Less 30% of Gross revenue for council tax, utilities, internet, voids etc

Net returns
15.71%

Can not get that in the bank can you?

http://www.bhinvestment.co.uk/

Commercial to Residential Money Machines

Andreas Panayiotou is a property tycoon sitting on approximately £400 million. He is the founder of the Ability Group and at one point he was one of the largest UK landlords. Panayiotou had a keen sense of the market and liquated his holdings prior to the crash in 2008. He was born in London to immigrant Cypriot parents. His family was in the dry cleaning business. He never really learnt to read and left school aged 14. This gent has more street smarts than all the so called professionals together.

Andreas was a former boxer whose career was cut short when his parents gave him a dry-cleaning shop in 1986. By the early 1990s he had built up a chain of six shops across north London. In 1992, he was offered a chance to buy a flat above one of his shops in Caledonian Road - which he renovated, sold and turned a £20,000 profit. After that, he purchased a property in Islington's Chapel Street Market, built four flats above it, and began renting them to local yuppies. Panayiotou was soon dubbed London's buy-to-let king, with almost 6,000 rental properties, including 600-unit apartment blocks in Canary Wharf and the West End in his portfolio.

He simply created value!

Andreas thinks out of the box. He probably was one of the first developers who converted commercial to residential. He is quoted as stating:

"We picked up schools, warehouses and old hospitals that no one knew what to do with. Areas like Hackney are now fashionable, but I was there years ago. You've got to go against the grain as an entrepreneur."

More so I respect how he leverages himself. He is quoted as

"I only borrow 55 per cent of the money to buy a property. Other property buyers will gear up to 90 per cent, which makes negative equity a problem for them."

As much he sold out in the 2007-2008 crash during other recessions, he purchased....He loved the falling prices.

As the deals got bigger he switched from fix 'em up jobs (commercial to residential) to new build. He bought the Abbey National on Baker Street, the one where Sherlock Holmes is supposed to live. That's now 140 flats.

To a much smaller degree....actually miniscule at this point, myself and my colleagues have worked on various commercial to residential projects.

They have included **office to residential**, a **store** (which had a fire) to a group of flats as well as a **warehouse project** which was to be flats however an investor came along and we sold the entire project.

Humphrey Street Warehouse to Residential

Humphrey street was a warehouse for antiques for decades. It was placed for auction however it failed to sell. It sat empty for quite sometime. One of my colleagues found it and thought we could convert to flats.

We approached the vendor and purchased it subject to having planning permission granted for an exact number of flats.

This is the original building

Even though the property was a warehouse it was in a heavily populated residential neighborhood. We called several estate agents and all told us the same story, ***there is a shortage of houses and flats***.

This was music to our ears.

We found a CAD designer to assist us with sketches of ideas of what the property would like once we finished. We were enthralled with the project.

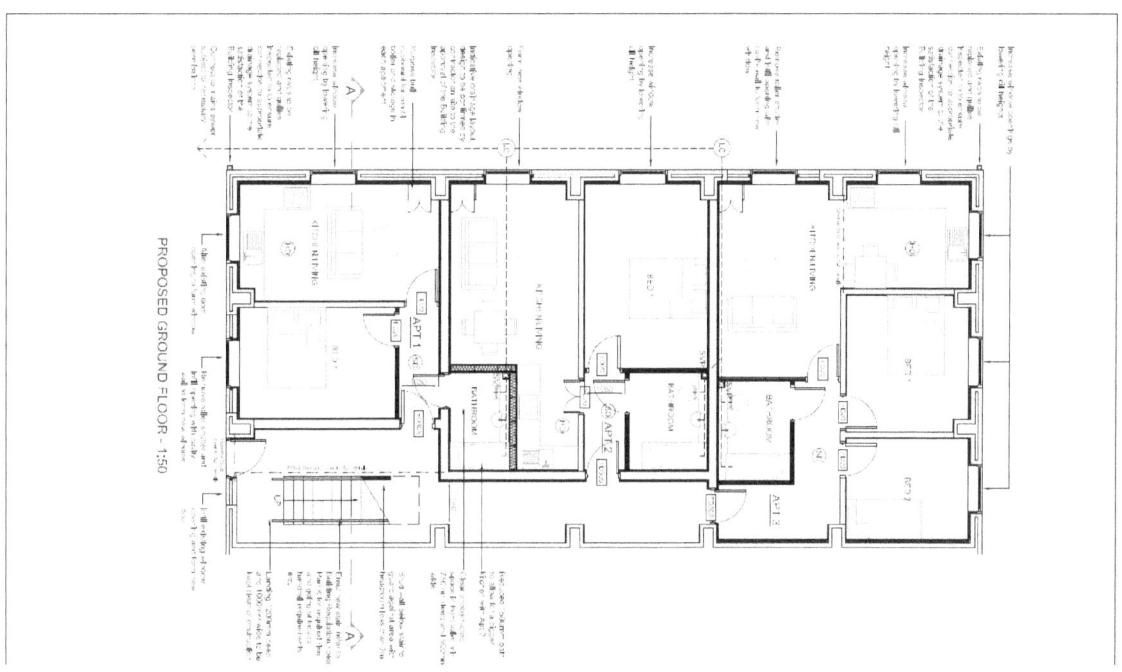

In this business you need to have imagination. These flats would be the nicest in the area and could command a higher rent.

Purchase of Humphrey Street

Completion Statement
Relating to the Purchase of Doric Cinema, Humphrey St, Wigan

Date: 19th January 2016
Ref: 1755.18/PO/JB/BHAAA

Monies Received

Funds on account from you	£5,900.00
Balance purchase funds from you	£54,234.10
Total Monies Received	**£60,134.10**

Monies Paid Out

Purchase Price of Property	£59,000.00
Local Authority, Drainage, Environmental and Coal Authority searches	£434.10
HMLR fee for pre-completion title searches	£3.00
HMLR fee SIM Search and Office Copies	£11.00
HMLR fee for registration of transfer and charge	£20.00
Redbird Conveyancing Limited Costs VAT and Disbursements	£666.00
Stamp Duty Land Tax	£0.00
Other Disbursements	£0.00
Total Monies Paid Out	**£60,134.10**

Sale Completion Statement

Completion Statement
Relating to the Sale of Doric Cinema, 2a Humphrey Street, Ince, Wigan WM2 2HS

Date: 13th May 2016
Ref : 1755.46/BHAAA

Monies Received

Sale Price of Doric Cinema	£115,000.00
ADD selling costs as per special condition 8.1.1. of auction contract	£750.00
Total Monies Received	**£115,750.00**

Monies Paid Out

Auction Fee	£1,470.00
Redbird Conveyancing Limited Costs VAT and Disbursements	£666.00
Total Monies Paid Out	**£2,136.00**
Balance Due To You	**£113,614.00**

E & OE

We took a quick profit on the conversion project and sold on to another investor as we had 5 other projects in the works.

Hyde Road Insurance office to a Block of Flats

Hyde road project was a shuttered insurance agency located in Tameside council . It was a fantastic location on a busy road with a straight shot into the city center. There was a massive Morrison's in a very close vicinity.

In every conversion project you need to have building regs submitted and approvals by the council. In some instances there is permitted development in the conversion or otherwise full planning is required. Full planning can be approximately 2 months however there might be need for revisions. Not an overly easy process if one has to go through full planning.

Building Regs

Economic Growth, Investment and Sustainability

ASHTON-UNDER-LYNE · AUDENSHAW · DENTON · DROYLSDEN · DUKINFIELD · HYDE · LONGDENDALE · MOSSLEY · STALYBRIDGE

BUILDING REGULATIONS CONDITIONAL APPROVAL NOTICE

The Building Act 1984
The Building Regulations 2010 (as amended)

Building Regulations
Reference 14/00699/OTH

Robin Monk
Executive Director

Planning and Building Control
Council Offices, Wellington Road
Ashton-under-Lyne, Tameside OL6 6DL

Call Centre 0161 342 8355
Fax 0161 342 2383
Minicom 0161 342 2283

www.tameside.gov.uk
Email: building.control@tameside.gov.uk

Details of works
Convert into 5no. Bed HMO

Location of building to which work relates
●● Hyde Road Denton Tameside M34 3AU

Conditional Approval
The plans submitted, including any amendments, in respect of the above work have been examined and passed by the Authority as complying with the Building Regulations subject to the conditions indicated on the attached schedule.

This conditional approval is only for the purposes of the requirements of the Building Regulations and Sections 16, 21, 24 and 25 of the Building Act 1984. It is not an approval under the Town and Country Planning Acts, an approval for improvement grant purposes or for any other statutory provision.

Under the requirements of the Building Regulations the person carrying out the work to which the Building Regulations relate is required to notify the Authority at certain stages during the execution of the work.

Town and Country Planning Act 1990

PLANNING PERMISSION

Name and address of applicant/agent:
Mr Anthony Hope
14 Pinfold Lane
Romiley
Stockport
SK6 4NP

Date of Application: 13th January

Date of Decision: 10th March 20

Application Number: 14/00025/FUL

Particulars of details submitted for approval:

Change of use from office (Use Class A2) to house (Use Class C3)

Hyde Road Denton Tameside M34 3AU

The Tameside Metropolitan Borough Council hereby gives notice that permission has been grant carrying out of the development referred to above, subject to the following conditions:

1. The development must be begun not later than the expiration of three years beginning wit of this permission.

2. During refurbishment/construction no work, including vehicle and plant movements, loading and unloading) shall take place outside the hours of 7.30 and 18.00 Mondays to F 08.00 to 13.00 Saturdays. No work shall take place on Sundays and Bank Holidays.

3. This permission relates to the submitted red edge plan received on 13th January 2013

4. Development shall not commence until the following information has been submitted in written permission at each stage has been granted by the Local Planning Authority.

Regarding Rents achievable

Local Housing Allowance Rates for the Tameside area is as follows:
One Bedroom Rate: £86.54 per week
Two Bedrooms Rate: £103.85 per week
Three Bedrooms Rate: £126.92 per week
Four Bedrooms Rate: £154.83 per week

Pictures of the Work

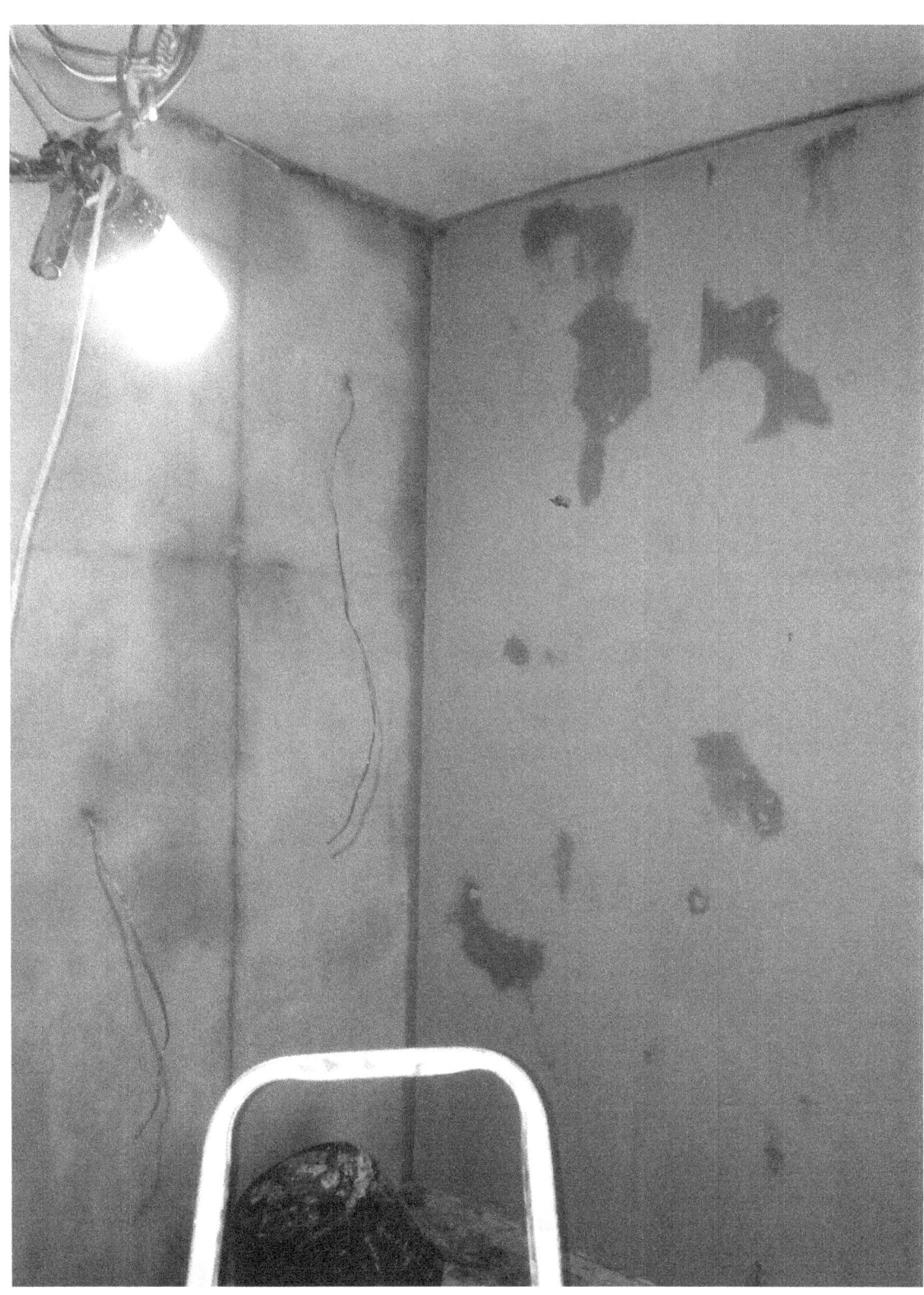

After Refurbishment

Hyde Road Purchase Statement

BHAAA1836 PROPERTY INVESTMENTS LTD IN ACCOUNT WITH GLAISYERS SOLICITORS LLP
RE: PURCHASE OF 61 HYDE ROAD DENTON
REF: JL/081300-02

COMPLETED 02.07.14	PAYMENTS	RECEIPTS
PURCHASE PRICE	63,500.00	
ADD		
BILL OF COSTS PURCHASE	425.00	
VAT THEREON	85.00	
BILL OF COSTS ADDITIONAL WORK INVOLVED RE CHANGE OF PURCHASING VEHICLE	100.00	
VAT THEREON	20.00	
SDLT RETURN FEE	50.00	
VAT THEREON	10.00	
BANK CHARGES	35.00	
VAT THEREON	7.00	
COAL SEARCH (COMMERCIAL)	95.22	
ENVIRO SEARCH (COMMERCIAL)	201.60	
MAPPING CHARGE	8.34	
HMLR SEARCH FEES	6.00	
HMLR REGISTRATION FEE	20.00	
TOTAL PAYMENTS:	**64,563.16**	

As the pictures above show there was a tremendous amount of time, money and energy in the refurbishment. We collected numerous of rents and sold the property on. Please note that we purchased way below market.

Completion Statement
Relating to the Sale of 61 Hyde Road

Date: 27th July 2015
Ref :   1755.15/PO/BHAAA

Monies Received

Sale Price of 61 Hyde Road	£160,000.00
Apportionment for rent through 27th July 2015	£905.81
Total Monies Received	**£160,905.81**

Monies Paid Out

HMLR fee for office copies and title plan X2	£12.00
HMLR fee for copy 1896 conveyance	£25.00
HMLR fee for copy 1923 conveyance	£25.00
HMLR fee for copy 1955 conveyance	£25.00
Redbird Conveyancing Limited Costs VAT and Disbursements	£606.00
Total Monies Paid Out	**£693.00**
Balance Due To You	**£160,212.81**

E & OE

Always being Creative Memorial Rd Worsley

As Andreas Panayiotou thinks out of the box, so do we.

"We picked up schools, warehouses and old hospitals that no one knew what to do with.

The Memorial Rd project was an eye sore in a lovely and desirable neighborhood of Manchester, Worsley. It was a store that was in a residential neighborhood which had a fire. Virtually no one wanted to touch this property. It sat on the market until my colleague whose greatest form of entertainment is searching for properties. He can sit on his apple computer with his organic this or that drink and not move for hours (maybe days).

He found this property and started negotiating.

I think you can imagine there was not a long list of potential buyers!

Before pictures

This property could have been a scene for a horror movie rather than a project of flats!!!

If you look closely, there was not even a floor!!!

After Pictures

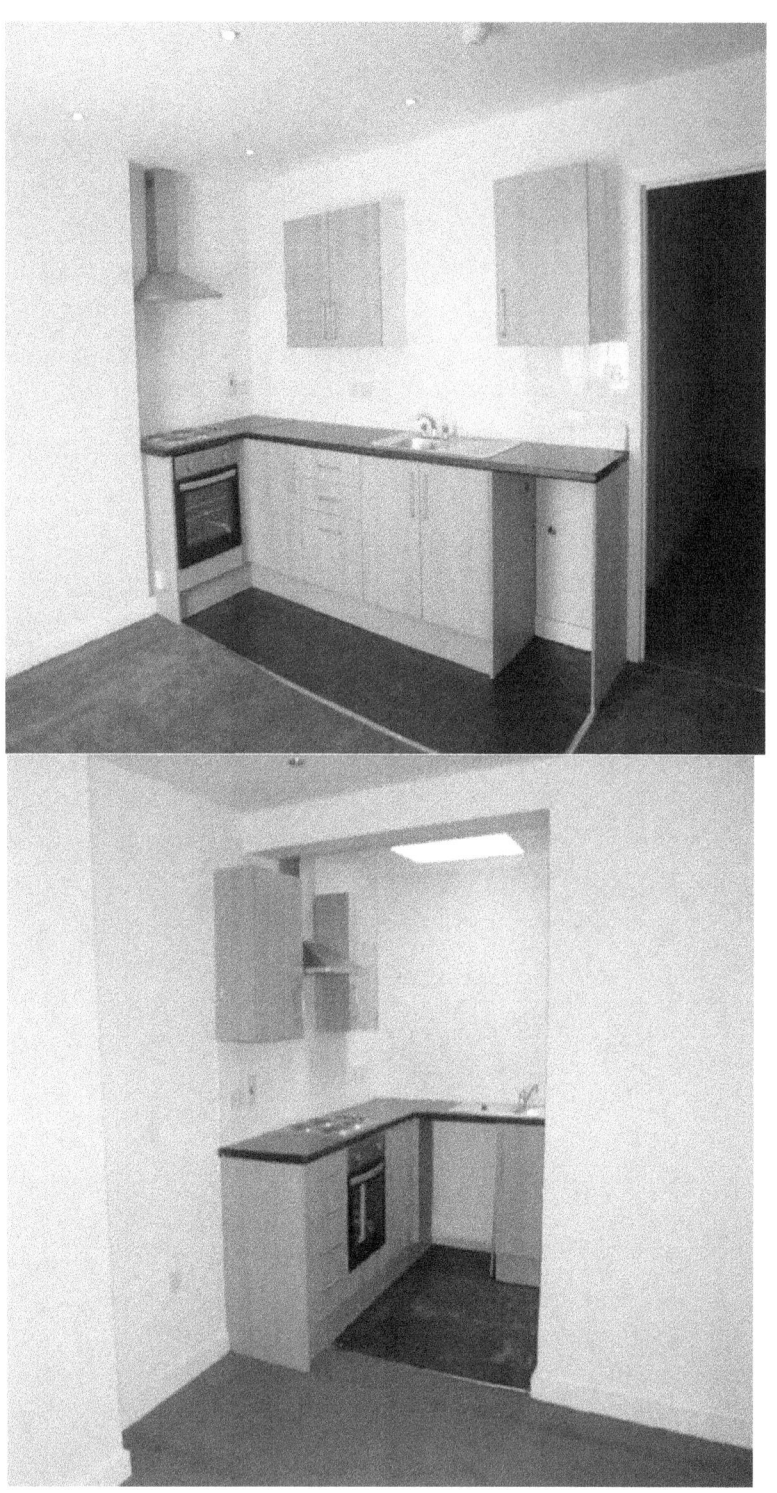

The icing on the cake of this deal was that we received a grant from Manchester council as we took an uninhabitable property and made it a group of quality flats. We did good for the council, the future tenants and us as business people!

Liz Treacy
City Solicitor
PO Box 532
Town Hall
Manchester
M60 2LA
(DX 714441 Manchester 1)

PROPERTY INVESTMENTS BH LTD
23 STOCKPORT ROAD
ASHTON –U-LYNE
OLDHAM
OL7 0LA

Date: 12 May 2015

RECORDED DELIVERY

Dear Sirs,

Property: 29 MEMORIAL ROAD, SALFORD, M28 3AG

Manchester and Salford Council's now operate a shared legal service and I act for Salford Council in this matter.

I am informed that a grant of up to £46,750.00 will be offered to you for the refurbishment of the above property which you would then lease to the Council as three flats for a 5 year period under the Empty Homes Programme.

I enclose the following documents based on the terms that I am informed have been agreed between yourselves and Salford Council's Empty Properties Team:

These profits were made before the Brexit. If there will be price reductions in real estate, would it be reasonable to assume profits are available for hard working hungry investors?

I would tend to believe there will be forced liquidations of real estate and more redundant properties on the market with a lack of financing. However I can be wrong as my crystal ball is not 100% of the time

http://www.bhinvestment.co.uk/

Joint Ventures in Real Estate

Throughout my real estate career I have never used bank finance. I have always used joint ventures to fund my deals or used our families money to provide for deals in which we JV with local investors. I had a bridging company in which we initially used our funds and within 6 months millions of dollars were put out on the street and we did not have further liquidity. I reached out to countless high net worth investors until after a period of time I established relationships with 5 well heeled investors. It was a wonderful relationship for all parties involved. They were 100% protected as they held first charges on properties in their perspective names or companies. I made money by sourcing and managing the deals.

Further more I did JV deals building houses and even a large warehouse project. One must be very careful whom they JV with. What is written on paper at the end of the day is rather meaningless. It is the integrity of the people and mostly at the end of the day, the investor must have control of the property, registered under their name or company.

We have completed on approximately 35 joint venture deals with our colleagues in Manchester. We have provided the finance for acquisition and for all the repairs. The property is titled in our company's name. If our JV partners do not fulfill their responsibilities outlined in the JV agreement they acknowledge they can be dismissed. However, I have found my JV partners hard working, motivated and fully committed. To exemplify the complete thoroughness, there was recently a document which needed original signatures. The document came to his office and he not only forwarded but provided an return envelope.

This is thoroughness!

When developing property, there are always issues. There can be (will be) electrical issues, plumbing issues and probably surprises along the way.

If you contemplate the approach of partnering via a JV. As much I am not giving investment advice nor legal, discuss first with your solicitor and financial advisor. Make sure the deal stacks up. Make sure your counterparties have experience and knowledge. Make your solicitor prepares the JV agreement and all your boxes are ticked.

A JV can be anything from a terraced house renovation to a HMO or to a significant project. After doing all your due diligence with your professionals (solicitor and financial advisor) start small. Test the waters.

This is exactly I started in Manchester with my JV partners. We did a simple 3 bed 2 reception house in Leigh (suburb of Manchester). My colleagues managed the renovation and tenanted the property virtually immediately. We split the rent 50/50 less their management fee. Now we are selling this property as we are focused on HMOs and bigger conversion projects.

Constellation House

We viewed this property and entered discussions with the vendor to purchase below the 200,000 asking price. The property was a redundant office. The roof needed a great of work. However we saw value. We deducted 10% off the size for hallways and common area. We figured we could put depending on what was granted via planning permission 14-18 flats. Rough cost per flat was 20,000-25,000 depending on the level of finish and numbers coming back from QS (Quantitative surveyor).

Unfortunately the vendor pulled this property off the market and decided to renovate and use for their corporate headquarters.

Rough Projections

Purchase price 180,000
SDLT   150,000 exempt
SDLT   600   30,000 @2%
Legal   2,000
Architect   10,000
Refurbishment 400,000 prior to approval assumption 16 flats @25,000 each subject to confirmation from approval of planning permission and QS

total rough cost 600,000 on the high side

16 flats rented @500 per month=96,000

10% Gross yield to an investor 960,000
Profit in less than 1 year 360,000

or sell to retail home buyers 70,000 (low side) 1,120,000 gross

Net 520,000

These numbers we try to over weight potential costs and underestimated sales price. Being conservative keeps you in business.

Redundant buildings like this are not overly complicated to find. Potentially in the post Brexit environment there will be many more.

Block Cherry Tree Hospital

Former Administration Block Cherry Tree Hospital, Dialstone Lane, Stockport
For Sale

Status: Available
Min. Size: 0.63 Acres

The property comprises a former hospital administration block which is a detached double storey period building of brick construction beneath a pitched slate roof. In addition there is some land to the rear of the property. The site has an area of approximately 0.63 acres (0.25 hectares). The existing building has an area of approximately 8,000ft^2.

Race Course Hotel

Race Course Hotel could have been an amazing project. A little out of our financial realm (in the short term). The asking price of this lovely project was in the vicinity of 300,000 however the refurbishment what upwards of 1,000,000. Roof work needed, outer facade needed plus all the interior work. However a project like this in Salford could make ones life once completed and tenanted.

Conclusion and Summary

"A pessimist sees difficulty in every opportunity; an optimist sees opportunity in every difficulty"

-Winston Churchill

Churchill's statement presents the idea that when there is great difficulty, there is often great value with significant upside potential. Discussed in the book earlier Benjamin Graham, Warren Buffet, J. Paul Getty, Sam Zell, John Templeton, Carlos Slim, and Li Ka-Shing, all had brilliant and bold instincts for distressed situations and bargain-priced assets.

Sam Zell built a $5 billion real estate empire buying deep-value real estate in down markets in the 1960s, and followed this strategy over the next forty years. John Templeton was a Rhodes Scholar, but it was his street-smart independent streak to scour the world for bargains – such as Japanese stocks that were ignored by everyone else in the 1960s – which made him a legend.

The Statement, that the only Certainty with the Brexit is the Complete Uncertainty is the underlying concept in this book. However in the uncertainty, in my personal opinion, when one purchases real estate below market value as I mentioned, the upside takes care of itself.

The options are truly limited in today's world. The Stock market has had a long run much longer than statistically bull markets have run. Thus increased risks. Stock are not cheap. Banks do not pay interest and their financial health is questionable. Bonds do not pay interest...

So what is left? **My personal answer is real estate.** Ask your financial advisors what they think. My personal answer is very clear.

If I can assist you or if you have any questions, please feel free to email me.

Andy Abraham
Info@Bhinvestment.co.uk
http://www.bhinvestment.co.uk/

www.ingramcontent.com/pod-product-compliance
Lightning Source LLC
Chambersburg PA
CBHW080617190526
45169CB00009B/3217